POP CULTURE INTO ART

NORMAN LAVERS

POP CULTURE INTO ART

THE NOVELS OF MANUEL PUIG

A LITERARY FRONTIERS EDITION, NO. 31

UNIVERSITY OF MISSOURI PRESS

COLUMBIA, 1988

Copyright © 1988 by
The Curators of the University of Missouri
University of Missouri Press, Columbia, Missouri 65211
Printed and bound in the United States of America

Library of Congress Cataloging-in-Publication Data

Lavers, Norman
        Pop Culture into art.
        (Literary frontiers edition)
        1. Puig, Manuel—Criticism and interpretation. 2. Popular
culture in literature. I. Title. II. Series.
ISBN 0-8262-0685-9 (alk. paper)

∞™ This paper meets the minimum requirements of
the American National Standard for Permanence of Paper
for Printed Library Materials, Z39.48, 1984.

FOR CHERYL AND GAWAIN

PREFACE

Since a number of new readers of Puig will have begun by seeing the movie *Kiss of the Spider Woman*, and from there will have gone on to read the novel by that name, and perhaps other of Puig's wonderful novels, it is a logical moment to bring out a book that analyzes certain aspects of the novels the reader will want to consider, and that also puts in the reader's hands the biographical information useful to have while reading Puig's fiction.

Puig has spoken freely and copiously in interviews about his early life and how it led into his novel writing, why he writes the special way he does, and what his intentions are. Some of these interviews are in English, but the great majority are in Spanish. I have made it a point in this book to quote extensively from the interviews in Spanish (the translations are mine) in order to make them available to those who do not read Spanish. In order to stave off certain kinds of criticism, I had better state here that I am not a professional Hispanist, and this is not a book written for specialists. I am a critic of current fiction who happens to read Spanish; this book is designed for the intelligent reader who does not. But I don't want to be too modest. Even the specialist will find much that is new in my readings of the novels. I have not, in this book, dealt with Puig's plays.

Though my friend George Chambers had long been insisting to me that I read Puig, I actually read him for the first time when an excerpt from *Kiss of the Spider Woman* appeared in the magazine *Fiction* (5, 2–3 (1978): 75–109). That aroused my enthusiasm sufficiently that when, thanks to an NEA grant, I had a leisurely year to spend in Mallorca, I ordered all his books in Spanish from a local bookstore and began a serious and delighted reading. A Faculty Summer Research Grant from my home institution, Arkansas State University, helped me through the final stages of research. For all of these I am grateful.

CONTENTS

WORKS BY MANUEL PUIG

In preparing my study, I have read these easily available paperback copies of Puig's novels. For each novel, I have given the English edition, followed by the Spanish edition. The date in parenthesis is the date of first publication in English or in Spanish, when it differs from the edition I read.

Betrayed by Rita Hayworth. New York: Avon, 1973 (1971).
La Traición de Rita Hayworth. Buenos Aires: Editorial
  Sudamericana, 1975 (1968).
Heartbreak Tango. New York: Vintage, 1981 (1973).
Boquitas Pintadas. Barcelona: Seix Barral, 1972 (1968).
The Buenos Aires Affair. New York: Vintage, 1980 (1968).
The Buenos Aires Affair. Barcelona: Seix Barral, 1977 (1973).
Kiss of the Spider Woman. New York: Vintage, 1980 (1979).
El Beso de la Mujer Araña. Barcelona: Seix Barral, 1976.
Pubis Angelical. New York: Vintage, 1986.
Pubis Angelical. Barcelona: Seix Barral, 1979.
Eternal Curse on the Reader of These Pages. New York: Vintage, 1983
  (1982).
Maldición Eterna a Quien Lea Estas Páginas. Barcelona: Seix Barral,
  1980.
Blood of Requited Love. New York: Vintage, 1984.
Sangre de Amor Correspondido. Barcelona: Seix Barral, 1982.

I. ART OUT OF
SCORNED OBJECTS

La obra era ésa, reunir objetos despreciados para compartir con
ellos un momento de la vida.

That was my work of art, to bring together scorned objects to
share with them a moment of life.

The Buenos Aires Affair

IT is more than usually helpful, in the case of a writer
like Manuel Puig, to know something of his background
and how he came to be a writer. Biographical details
neatly explain his techniques, his themes, and, particularly, his materials. It is especially in his materials that we
see one of the most unique characteristics of this entirely
unique novelist: his use of debased or subliterary forms of
language and art—the tango and bolero, the soap opera,
the detective story, serial fiction, the *fotonovela*, and,
above all else, the Hollywood movie.

"El fenómeno Puig," the great reception Puig's novels have received in Latin America and the critical attention that is accorded them—almost as much is written
about Puig each year as is written about García Már-
quez—has been a fact of Latin American literary life since
his first book was published in 1968. In the United States
at least since the mid–1970s Puig has been a favorite of
avant-garde writers and readers, and all of his novels are
available in English translation. But it was not until the
success of the award-winning movie made from his novel
Kiss of the Spider Woman that he received the wide attention
in this country that his unique but quite accessible novels
deserve.

Puig, like the characters in his first two novels, was
born (in 1932) in a flat, dusty, landscapeless town in the
Argentine pampas. The setting was not only physically
ugly but also morally oppressive, with its ethic of unre-

1

mitting machismo. Those too sensitive to flourish in such an environment escaped to the town's movie theater to merge and identify with and to shape their dreams from the images of 1930s and 1940s Hollywood films. Ultimately for these sensitive ones (Puig among them) the movies became reality, and the harsh life of the town outside the theater became a B movie they had been placed in through an error in casting.

Puig himself was thirty years old before he escaped the enchantment sufficiently to turn back and write about it in his extraordinary novels, which are compassionate at the same time that they miss absolutely nothing. In the bleak pampas the institutionalized oppression—boys over girls, men over women, a dictator over the state— was laid bare, but when his novels left the pampas and moved into the centers of civilization they found the same oppression there, but everywhere concealed and at the same time reinforced by the anodyne popular culture of tangos, soap operas, and Hollywood films. It is not a surprise that *Kiss of the Spider Woman* should be so popular as a film. It may be his best novel as well, at least insofar as it has captured all his themes within the most perfect imaginable metaphor: two men literally imprisoned by their culture, in this case in the penitentiary in Buenos Aires, who, with a constant threat of torture and destruction hanging over them, must face each day the annihilating monotony of their incarceration. It is Puig's version of *Waiting for Godot*. To pass the time, one tells lovingly remembered plots of Hollywood films to the other, and this becomes their necessary reality—even though in subtle ways the films are the purest expression of what has imprisoned them.

Perhaps biography explains Puig's sources too neatly. What we know about his origins comes chiefly through his remarks in numerous interviews. I do not mean to suggest he is mythologizing his past, but in his insistence on casting himself as a naif who fell into his extraordinary novel-writing techniques by chance and force of circumstances there may a degree of simplification. When he

2

speaks of himself as timid and feckless it must be kept in mind that he is a sophisticated world citizen, fluent in five languages (he has written novels in three), that he studied film directing with De Sica and screenwriting with Zavattini, and that in all his writing and his discussions of his writing he shows himself to be an extremely self-conscious artist and technician. Still, as Henry James said, if you give an artist an inch, he will take an ell, so it is quite possible simple causes fashioned richly proliferating and almost instantaneous results in his waiting sensibility.

The first detail to know about him is that his background is not literary. He insists on that. Now that he is a figure in Latin American literature, there is some effort being made to show how he fits into it—but if he does fit, it is in the sense of Eliot's "Tradition and the Individual Talent," where the individual writer alters the whole of the preceding tradition in order to make his place in it. The truth is that Manuel Puig is not like any other Latin American writer. He knows the other writers now, has met them in conferences, and no doubt has read some of their books. But this was not the case when he was starting. He did not then esteem literature highly—he still does not read much fiction. He did not read literature written in Spanish, and most certainly he did not read literature from his native Argentina. He gives his reasons:

I was born in a town in the pampas where life was very hard, very difficult—almost like the *Far West*. The prestige of strength. No one questioned machismo. Authority had the most prestige possible. . . . These were the coordinates. Weakness, sensibility, had no prestige. A world I rejected.[1]

Rejecting this world meant, for him, rejecting its literature: "I had read all the Italian classics when I studied Italian, the French . . . but the Spanish . . . was all colored by the pampas, by the machismo I had rejected" (Sosnowski, 72).

That does not mean his background was not artistic, only that another form held dominance. "For me literature was a secondary thing . . . like listening to music, like looking at a painting. . . . All my expectations, all my attention, was on movies" (Sosnowski, 70).

It is worth examining the psychology of his relationship to movies, because it influences the shape of his writing, and because it penetrates the psychology of his characters.

> In this town there was *one* means of escaping reality: movies. One single theater that gave a different picture every day. I went with mama at least four times a week. Little by little I changed the terms: that which was reality changed into a class Z movie in which I had been stuck by mistake. Reality . . . was what happened in the movies, not what happened in town, which was a western from Republic. (Sosnowski, 69)

Since movies meant everything to him it seemed natural, when it came time for him to choose a career, to try to enter the movie-making industry. The way to enter the world of the movies, he felt, was through language. This meant, preeminently, English, since that was the language of the Hollywood films he most esteemed. He learned French also, and latterly Italian, since in the period we are talking about, right at the end of the Second World War, the Italian neorealist film was gaining prestige. Puig had nothing but contempt for the undeveloped Argentine film industry. So he studied these languages, and won a scholarship in 1956 to study at Cinecittà in Rome.

He was immediately disenchanted. Instead of finding a beautiful world of technicolor and romantic love, a place of saints like Norma Shearer, a place where sensibility always triumphed, he found the same power-jockeying, the same prestige for authority and for nothing else. Even directing was simply another kind of exploitation, of forcing one's will on another. As an escape from this, in his free time he began coming at movies from the direction of screenwriting. Significantly, he wrote not in his rejected Spanish but in the English of Hollywood.

4

I knew English pretty well, but not well enough to write in. . . . For me English was the language of film. This first screenplay was a "sophisticated comedy" of the thirties written in 1958, a time of total derision for the thirties. I wrote it with great enthusiasm. While I was writing it I felt good. When I finished it, I didn't. It was an abortion. Horrible. . . . What I had wanted was to prolong my times as an infantile spectator. To rewrite some movie that had really impressed me, but it cost me three screenplays to find that out. Naturally I didn't sell them. . . . I realized that what I enjoyed in making films was copying. Creating didn't interest me at all. What I wanted was to re-make things from another epoch, things already seen. To recreate the moment in childhood in which I had felt safe in the dark hall. (Sosnowski, 70–71)

The situation was serious. When he was a child in a small town in the pampas, everything was regulated by power, by machismo, and no esteem was given to sensibility, which was the only thing the boy had. When he went to secondary school and to the university in the big city, in Buenos Aires, he expected everything to be different. But he found it was just the same thing again, the same power and authority, the same exploitation of the weak. His escape had always been the movies, but when he finally arrived in Italy and got inside the fabled precincts themselves, he found it was once more the same thing.

I was in Rome, thirty years old, without career, without money, and discovering that the vocation of my whole life—cinema—had been an error, a neurosis and nothing more. (Sosnowski, 71)

Friends of his, who were far enough outside his problem to have some perspective on it, saw why his screenplays were failing. They counseled him to write in his native language and to write about things he knew, something particular that he had experienced.

I tried to write a screenplay about the loves of cousin in my town. It was autobiographical material that was deep inside

5

me and that I couldn't see with the necessary distance. To make the characters clearer to me I decided to make, before the dialogue, before shaping the plot, etc., a small description of each one to make them clear to me. These descriptions weren't to show to anybody . . . They were, for the first time, in Spanish. How to do it? I didn't know how to describe characters. I didn't find the vocabulary. But I remembered the voice of an aunt. Her voice came to me very clearly, things this woman had said while washing clothes, while cooking, twenty years before. I began to record that voice. The description that was going to be two pages ended up being thirty. It was material that flowed by itself. I quickly realized that the voice I heard was material that I could handle. In spite of the fact that I was returning to a reality I had rejected, I was interested in going on with it. It ended up as a kind of interior monologue. (Sosnowski, 71)

I think we must believe Puig when he tells us he had rejected the experience of his childhood so utterly that he had even rejected his own language. And thus we must see it as a psychological as well as an artistic breakthrough when in his desperation he was able to return to both the experience and the language in which it was cast. Having freed himself from the blockage, he could free himself also from the device he had used to escape the misery of his childhood.

After two or three days I realized it was literary, not cinematographic, material, that I could revise it, that I could remake it, that there were no deadlines, no authority there. . . . It was a thing I could do in tranquillity. I liked these working conditions. I went from one character to the next. . . . I had eight interior monologues. Thus began my first novel, *Betrayed by Rita Hayworth*. (Sosnowski, 71)

The movies had been an escape, "a neurosis and nothing more," but when he fell suddenly into novel writing, there is no sign that it was simply a new escape to replace the original, failed escape. There is no more blindness, no more unrealistic expectation. Immediately he is making artistic decisions, immediately he is making realistic assessments of his strengths and his weaknesses.

> I didn't know how to do anything but write interior monologues because pure Spanish made me tremble. The only thing I wanted to do was register voices. But I wasn't just a recorder. Afterward I manipulated the material, I cut it . . . I did any experiments I liked with it, but the material was always the spoken language. . . . But in the interior monologues . . . there came a certain moment when I began to repeat myself. I needed some other techniques. Third person was not possible, because my Spanish was lost, I had no confidence in it [he had been out of Argentina for eight years]. I didn't even have any reading material in Spanish. . . . I needed something that was neither interior monologue nor third person. Then it came to me . . . : casual writing, that is to say, people writing, people who could commit errors writing. I figured if I knew the psychology of the character, I could make him write. I had these characters write letters, intimate diaries, scholarly compositions, and in this way completed the novel escaping third person. (Sosnowski, 71–72)

Puig was not simply, however, avoiding the difficulty of third person. He quickly perceived the utility of what he was doing.

> I was not only afraid to use third person, but I also didn't feel it was an instrument adequate for the work I wanted to do. I was especially interested in characters I knew in my childhood who handed over to me their secrets, their intimacy. I had lots of facts about them but one can never know the totality of a person. One can try to reconstruct it in some way, but I was not too sure about being able to reconstruct them, although it occurred to me that listening to them speak or having them write a letter, they alone were going to reveal themselves to me. (Sosnowski, 72)

Puig was in fact reinventing the novel. There is an uncanny similarity between his words and those of the first inventor of the modern novel, Samuel Richardson. Richardson also was a sensitive, precociously intelligent,

7

perhaps effeminate young boy to whom people confessed their intimate secrets. At a young age Richardson began writing letters for serving girls who could not write themselves, and he learned that sometimes when they wrote to their boyfriends they wanted their words to say one thing but their tone to say another. He learned, in short, the indirect ways in which the soul revealed its truth. When he began to write *Pamela*—and Richardson too was a very self-conscious artist knowing exactly what he was doing— he developed his famous epistolary style, remembering that a person's own writing could reveal the truth of his soul more subtly and more complexly than pages of authorial description in the third person.

So it is a pleasant irony. What seems so new, so modern in Puig, what makes the first and strongest impression on the reader, Puig's extreme objectivity, his refusal to appear as narrator, is in fact the oldest and first trick of the novel genre, forgotten by succeeding generations of writers, and reinvented by Puig in almost the same way that it first was. I don't mean for a moment to say that Puig is not original. Precisely what the truly original artist does is to reinvent his form, recast it with the stamp of his freshness and uniqueness.

Although virtually all of Richardson's fictions are cast in the form of exchanges of letters, Richardson, as did Puig, recognized the need for polyphony. In the letters one finds monologue, third-person narrative, in moments of stress something close to stream-of-consciousness, and very often scenes of almost pure dialogue (Richardson was strongly influenced by Restoration and eighteenth-century drama, just as Puig was influenced by Hollywood movies). But Puig has shown much more interest in the effects of putting different kinds of writing and different narrative styles side by side. At least here he concedes that he had a literary influence.

I have never read *Ulysses* all the way through. In truth, all I did was peruse it. I haven't even read all of Molly Bloom's

8

monologue. But what I saw in the book was the immense free-dom, which was very stimulating, very liberating to me. I learned that there was no need to tell the story with just one technical device.[2]

Puig's own telling of how he became a novelist can lead to a suggestion that everything happened by default, that he had no aesthetic control over material that, in fact, simply wrote itself. But such a conclusion annoys him, as it annoyed Richardson. Richardson was at some pains to describe the artistic use he made of his materials, the indi-rect way he revealed the psychology of his characters, the suspense he created by having his characters writing "to the moment," when they themselves did not know the outcome. Puig too insists on his aesthetic control.

To live in terms of beauty, that's what I wanted. What helped me in literature was that I could put both things together—reality and beauty. If not in life, at least in literature. For myself at least, my books are always investigations, researches, certain ways of looking at problems that are mine, and not only mine, I hope. That research, however, has to be done with an esthetic rigor. The reality must be recreated and sustained at the same time and analyzed at the same time by a wish to create beauty. Beauty, in this case, is form.

RC: Many readers seem to have missed the point of the form.

MP: That happened with my first two novels. With the third I got a little more respect. People would say, oh, those books are just taped records of reality; you went out into the streets and recorded the voices of the people, that's all. That made me furious. Even if the characters' voices were the only material—and they were not—I was "editing" them just as other writers edit cultured, written language. This was a mat-ter that I had made clear to myself from the first day that I started to write literature: the fact that I was dealing with real-ity wasn't enough; reality had to be told in terms of beauty, otherwise there was no satisfaction for me. (Christ, 55–56)

His original priority had been beauty and escape from the sordidness of reality. Later he still wanted the beauty, but he wanted to create it out of reality, out of the sordidness, out of those things he had rejected. There was at least in part a kind of therapeutic reason.

> I always start with an obsession, a subject that haunts me, that I need to develop. Such subjects are problems of my own that I can't deal with consciously—personal problems. And I feel relieved if I develop the subject as a story. Once I have that subject, I look for the best shape to give it. (Christ, 52)

The neurotic solution, which failed him, had been to escape from reality through the beauty of Hollywood movies. The healthy solution, which now sustains him, is to come to terms with reality by converting it into beauty. Here indeed we are close to the center of Puig's art, and close to unraveling the theme that runs through each of his works. All of Puig's characters, just as Puig was himself, are faced with the sterility, the cruel oppression, of their lives. This life is the given; there is no escape from it (there is nowhere else to go), there is only the illusion of escape. Therefore, if their lives are not to be rendered meager and meaningless, the characters must redeem themselves, and they can only do so by rearranging the sordid and banal terms of their reality, converting them somehow into meaning and beauty. Puig has shown one way, converting the vulgarity of language, the sentimental banality and deceit of subliterature and other forms of popular culture, into his fine novels. At thirty he measured his life a failure, because he still had not learned to do this, so it is no wonder that thirty is often a critical age in the lives of his characters, and it is not surprising he feels compassion for those who fail. When they do succeed, however, it is not because they have spurned the materials they had to work with, but because they have somehow transcended them.

Often it is because they have become, as Puig became, *bricoleurs.* A number of commentators have made the connection between Puig's techniques and the idea of bricolage advanced by Claude Lévi-Strauss.[3] Lévi-Strauss was distinguishing between primitive science and modern science. Whereas a modern scientist creates new tools and materials to engineer a solution to problems, a primitive scientist makes use of what is preexistent in his world to improvise solutions. Lévi-Strauss took the term *bricoleur* for that early scientist, because in modern French the term refers to a sort of odd-jobs man who can make or fix anything from whatever materials are at hand. The key point is that in solving problems he never uses new materials specifically acquired for the job, but limits himself to these things at hand. The materials at hand are the cast-off ready-mades of society, but through recombining them he transcends and redeems their cast-off quality. There is not much profit in trying to compare Puig to a primitive scientist, but the term *bricoleur,* once it is mentioned, is so exactly descriptive of Puig's methods that I want to retain it. Gladys, the artist in *The Buenos Aires Affair,* has a life that parallels Puig's in many ways. She too at thirty is at a stall, having failed in life, having taken all the wrong turns.

That night I felt lonelier than ever. Imprisoned by despair I returned to the cottage and, almost crazed, I had an inspiration. I couldn't sleep. At five the dawn found me on the beach, for the first time picking up the debris that the surf had left on the sand. Flotsam, I only dared to love flotsam, anything else was too much to dare hope for. I returned home and began to talk . . . with a discarded slipper, with a bathing cap in shreds, with a torn piece of newspaper, and I started to touch them and to listen to their voices. That was my work of art, to bring together scorned objects to share with them a moment of life, or life itself.[4]

Lévi-Strauss says, "Further, the 'bricoleur' also, and indeed principally, derives his poetry from the fact that he does not confine himself to accomplishment and execution: he 'speaks' not only *with* things, as we have already seen, but also through the medium of things: giving an account of his personality and life by the choices he makes between limited possibilities" (p. 21). Jorgelina Corbatta,

11

in an interview with Puig, quotes the passage from *The Buenos Aires Affair* I have just given, concerning Gladys on the beach making her collages, and connects it to Lévi-Strauss's *bricolage*. Corbatta asks Puig, "What relationship exists between all this and your concept of art?" Puig replies, "I share totally Gladys's concept of art."[5]

Who were the people whose voices Puig remembered, and what was the language they spoke and wrote in, and why were they so completely trapped by the shoddiest parts of their culture?

It is necessary to remember that in Argentina, the great mass of the population was formed at the beginning of the century and was formed by immigrants (peasants who speak Galician, Catalan, Basque, Italian, Polish). These immigrants wanted to enter the middle class, to be small merchants, employees, and they couldn't pass any cultural heritage to their children, they couldn't even pass on a language. These children had to learn Spanish in the streets: everything in the house was "dubious," nothing in the house served because it was already superceded; so the models of language handy were those of the songs, those of the cheap press, those of the serials that circulated at that time, and were always a language "highly charged," an unreal language, high-sounding, too florid. The language of the tango, for instance. Why is the language of the tango always so truculent? Because it was directed at very simple people, who you have to impress with effects, and which, in some ways, is a language difficult to repeat because it is not real. The Argentine, then, the Argentine of the first generation and his children, sees that there is a language of the home that includes dialectal forms, and that is spontaneous, and another, a language of the street, that one uses when the time comes to express yourself: a declaration of love, writing a letter, discussing something at a bar. (Corbatta, 616–17)[6]

As I have worked much with the language of my characters, I have had, of necessity to work with the songs of the period, with the radio of the period, big influences on the language of these characters. . . . This first generation had a little to invent a language; they had to seize whatever models were at hand. The models closest were the radio, the songs, the tango;

in the forties the boleros from Mexico and Cuba; the subtitles of American films and very much the women's magazines, the fashion magazines. (Sosnowski, 80)

Puig is in no way parodying or being satirical of these characters. If their language is inadequate, it is not through a fault in the characters, but because this is the language the culture has given them to live their lives in, to express their deepest feelings in, to have their thoughts and dreams in.

JL: In "The Streetcorner Man" Borges caricatures the language of lower class people from the point of view of a cultured person. Manuel empathizes with the first-generation Argentinians living in the pampas and therefore treats their language differently. Yet there is a similarity between the two writers, in the sense that both of them *reveal* language. They make you conscious or aware of it; they both parody language through a conscious burlesque of it.

MP: But I hate the word "parody"; I think it is misleading. I'm often embarrassed when someone says to me: "You mock the way poor people speak." That isn't my intention, and I'm sorry if it comes out that way. The point is that the ordinary speech of these people is already a parody. All I do is record their imitation. This is why I think the word "parody" may lead people to the wrong conclusion.[7]

Perhaps it is for this reason that Puig, in many statements, has denied satiric or parodic intent of any kind. But the truth is that his attitude toward his materials is shifting and complex. In Juan Carlos's obituary notice in *Heartbreak Tango,* or in the opening passages of *The Buenos Aires Affair* or *Pubis Angelical,* Puig is clearly having fun parodying subliterary language. When he casts his novels in the form of serials or detective thrillers he claims that he means to be redeeming these useful forms for literature, but in fact he has altered the forms so greatly for his purposes that the real audience for those forms would put down his novels in puzzlement after the first few pages.

The form of popular culture with the most far-reaching effects on Puig himself, of course, is the Hollywood movie. We will see in later chapters how directly important movies are as materials in his novels, as influences on the lives of his characters, providing them not only a language but also a mode of living, a mark to aspire for, a pattern for values, a metaphor, however unreliable, for life. But in less overt ways movies provide formal patterns for Puig's writing and structuring. His professional training, after all, is in the movies.

> I don't have obvious literary models, because, I think, there are no great literary influences in my life. This space is filled by the influence of the movies. I believe that if someone took the trouble he might find influences of Lubitsch in certain of my structures, of Von Sternberg in this love of certain atmospheres. A lot of Hitchcock. . . . (Corbatta, 596)

> I believe there are affinities with Von Sternberg, with *Dishonored* by Von Sternberg. It is a picture that, when I see it—ay! how close he is to what I am doing! (Corbatta, 601)

When Puig was asked if he kept his reader in mind when he was writing, he said:

> I always have the readers before me. I write for a reader with my limitations. A reader with certain difficulties concentrating on reading, which, in my case, proceeds from my formation as a watcher of movies. Therefore I try not to ask for special strengths of attention on the part of the reader.
> JC: But don't you think these switches, these parallel stories or the same story told on different levels, causes . . . ?
> MP: It causes reflection, that is another kind of mental operation. For me what is hardest is to follow a story that has no determined thread. . . . I don't mean I am thinking of a stupid reader but of a reader with a certain need for speed. I believe that the movies are this, before all, that they have provoked in us a need for speed. (Corbatta, 592–93)

> I wouldn't say I was mad about the movies of today. The movies of today are not much interested in "story telling" . . .

and this is the part that's interesting, the art of narration. This is what the movies of today don't do, and the movies of the thirties did do. (Sosnowski, 77)

Indeed, though he came at it in his own way, his attitude and his practice are not dissimilar to many modern innovative writers—Borges, Hawkes, Kosinski, to name a few—who exploit the techniques and materials of sub-literary genres—detective fiction, pornography, spy thrillers, and so on. These writers both parody and profit by the sensational materials and strong plotting of such forms, just as the reader in part keeps an amused ironic detachment and in part enjoys the sex and violence on the lowest level. What is special about Puig is that the popular culture gives him not only forms and materials to utilize but also his themes. One theme, developing more and more clearly as Puig continues writing and thinking, is first how this secondhand culture strangles and destroys his characters and finally how that culture is manipulated by a self-serving state to hold its citizens in thrall. The popular culture is a sinister net, and it is frightening how few of his characters slip through it, even momentarily, and horrifying how the culture seeks to take revenge on them when they do.

Yet some few can wrest, even out of the destructive materials themselves, a few moments of salvation. It will be my theme in this book to see how Puig as novelist, and his characters as creators of their own lives, take the degraded, secondhand, ready-made materials of their world (bricoleurs by necessity) and try to create with them moments of beauty. The stakes are mortal, the success rate is low. But—so miraculous is the human spirit—it is higher than a first reading of the novels might suggest.

II. BETRAYED BY
RITA HAYWORTH

Como él tiene una cara perfecta, las invita a adjudicarle un
alma perfecta.

Since he had a perfect face, he invited them to judge he also
had a perfect soul.

Manuel Puig, interviewed by Reina Roffé

WHEN you begin reading *Betrayed by Rita Hayworth*
(1968), Puig's first novel, you are at once struck by the technique—struck by it because at first it causes confusion.
Voices are speaking, but there is no "he said" or "she said,"
there is no explanation of who is speaking, of what people
are present, of how they are related. The conversation does
not begin at the beginning. It is merely ongoing, shifting,
with people entering or leaving the room. The effect is as if
you were walking down a street and stopped, just out of
sight, by an open window and eavesdropped on those
within. You see nothing, but you hear the voices clearly. It is
someone's life unfolding. Your interest has been aroused,
and you listen closely, trying to work out the relationships,
trying to gain some insight into these chance-encountered
lives.

It is Puig's famous objective technique, the narrator
so thoroughly erased he will not even tell you who is
speaking. In the preceding chapter we read Puig's explanations for how he came to write in this way, how his lack
of a literary background and uncertainty about his facility
with his own language inhibited him from writing in a
conventional third person. Also he felt diffident about
trying to interpret the characters, uncertain if he really
knew enough about them. He felt certain only that he
could, with his fine ear, record the voices of people he
remembered, because his characters were always based

on real people, or combinations of people, to whom he had once listened. Add to this that Puig was trained as a director's assistant and as a screenwriter, and so he was used to working with screenplays, which in effect are a kind of pure dialogue.

That is the reason he came to write in this way, but that doesn't prepare us for the impact of his style. At first, as I have said, it is disorienting, because the author gives us no help. We have to cling to every word, straighten out relationships for ourselves, interpret for ourselves what is significant in the ongoing rush of ordinary language about cooking and sewing and housecleaning. It is as though Puig has presented us with the raw material, unsorted, of human life, and we are the artists, we are the ones on whom, as Henry James exhorted the artist, nothing should be lost.

It is all deceit on the author's part, of course. Naturally everything is pre-sorted and significant, with only enough talk of cooking and sewing to give the illusion of casual conversation.[1] But the effect is that we have an overwhelming sense of the reality of these characters, of the truth of these lives.

The effect is achieved because our minds, seeing everything from the outside, as it were, unmediated by the author, have been forced to operate in a way parallel to the way they operate when we are trying to sort out situations or evaluate people in real life. Puig is not the first to have seen the advantage of writing in this fashion.[2] What is special about Puig is how much further he goes with his objective technique than other writers. It was a cliché of nineteenth-century realistic fiction that the best art was the art that concealed itself, the art that made you laugh or made you cry without your being aware of the tricks the writer used in achieving his effects. Puig is not quite writing in this tradition. He is writing to a very sophisticated reader, and while he wants to have the effect of—to use E. M. Forster's term—"bouncing" the reader into belief in his characters (some of the most convincing characters in recent fiction) he also wants the reader to recognize and to enjoy his techniques, his aesthetic skills. So he is *more* objective, strictly speaking, than he needs to be; the dialogue is less mediated, more confusing, than is strictly necessary to give us the effect of seeing everything from the outside. In fact, he calls attention to his techniques, wanting us to see and to appreciate them. "I would like to say something about the objective narrative. I think that all the efforts an author makes to be objective are hopeless. So here I just wanted to take objectivity to its limits to show how impossible it is. This is really a kind of joke, you see" (Levine, 38).

There are three points, then, to consider. First, there is our aesthetic pleasure in enjoying Puig's skillful use of his objective form, which he overdoes enough to make certain he brings our attention to it. Second, there is the compelling reality of his characters, because we as readers, with our hard creative work, have ourselves brought them to life in our imaginations. Third, because we see the world only through the words of the characters, and because their only vocabulary is the secondhand one they have inherited from popular culture, we are trapped with them in their semiotic prison. It is because we must inhabit their world that we feel no sense of satire or ironic distance when the most moving, decisive, and dangerous moments of their lives are shaped and governed by the words of tangos, the plots of soap operas and Hollywood movies.

It is especially appropriate in *Betrayed by Rita Hayworth* that the characters be foregrounded in this way, because in this novel it is enough for the reader to see the characters and their relationships in order to comprehend fully the novel. Let me demonstrate.

As we continue to eavesdrop on these ordinary people we begin to put things together. The date at the beginning of the novel is 1933. A child has recently been born. Puig we know was born in 1932, and he has told us in many interviews that he is that child ("este chico, que soy yo"; Sosnowski, 72), the parents are his parents, and the others are the people he knew in his childhood growing up in a small town in the pampas. These are the first-generation immigrants and their children that he told us about. The infant's father, Berto, is a Catalan, with family still living in Barcelona. The mother, Mita, has parents who came over from Italy and still have connections there. Puig (whose name is Catalan) spoke once of his own parents:

> There was a couple—a woman very educated, a degree, who came to the city, very alert, very experienced, married with a man who didn't have the education she did, but who had another kind, and had other virtues: he was a man of great imagination. . . . For some reason, this woman who had education could not demonstrate it because she had taken the role of a submissive woman, at the same time that the man, who was very insecure (because anyone with imagination is unable to be secure, a thousand possibilities occurring to him at each step, in each situation) had taken the role of the secure macho. (Corbatta, 617)

In the novel, Mita has her degree in pharmacy, whereas her husband, Berto, was forced to quit school at fifteen to work for his brother in a factory. We learn about him chiefly through the long letter he writes to his brother in Spain, and never mails, a letter full of resentments, but ones he could never express because he does not really know how to express his inner feelings. The society has not given him the appropriate models to express them. The society has given him a pre-digested culture of machismo to be expressed in the vocabulary of the tangos and boleros and the subtitles of Hollywood films in which men powerfully dominate the world and all the women in it, while the women wait for them submissively at home. But Berto's real character comes through between the lines of his letter. He is completely in love with his wife and child, and he wants to give them everything. This to excess, because it has left him overworked and exhausted, constantly plotting how to get ahead and worrying when he does not, and therefore bad-tempered when he would be affectionate. What comes through most clearly is his domesticity. Since marrying, he has never glanced at another woman and, given his choice, would never leave his house. He is able to express none of this, and because of his anxiety over making money he is almost never present to his family, so that in effect young Toto grows up without any sense of having a father.

Mita got her degree in pharmacy, but that, she says, was not what she wanted, it was what her parents forced her into. She wanted to go to the school of liberal arts, and she still spends all her time reading novels. Her family, thinking she had read enough already to last several lifetimes, are astonished with her, because she went on reading books even after she got her degree. She is ambitious for something—she doesn't know what. Thinking about the movie version of "Romeo and Juliet," she wonders, if they awoke in time, so they could live happily ever after, what would they do? Just sit around the house having children? There must be something more. Perhaps she might have been a scholar, or a writer, or even a practicing pharmacist. Instead she has some lesser job in the hospital, and Berto's plan is that he will eventually make enough for her to quit any kind of work and stay home and have babies. The two do the best they can with the values their culture has given them, with the language deriving from the popular culture. But that language does not enable them to tell each other what they want.

Most salient in the popular culture—disguised by romantic language—is machismo: the male is secure and dominant; the female is submissive and takes a lesser role. Berto and Mita have tried to live their lives accordingly, but it is a bad fit with their real natures. He is unhappy, anxious, bad-tempered, dyspeptic, and worst of all estranged from his family. She is distant from him, frustrated, and lives increasingly in Hollywood movies and romantic novels, living her aesthetic life vicariously through her son.

Toto the son is timid and effeminate. Berto would love him, but the role of macho foisted on him tells him he must instead be disappointed by him, and so—denying what is probably real fellowship of feeling—he tries to force the macho version of manhood on Toto. This is unacceptable to Toto, and father and son are pushed further and further apart. The mother perhaps overly protects her son and draws out his precocious love of art. It is a classic study of the development of homosexuality.

Here is where, in the first instance, the popular culture has played them false. Berto and Mita would have been happier, more generous, more fulfilled people if their roles had been reversed. But the roles of men and women are rigorously and unceasingly dictated by every aspect of the popular culture, most insidiously by the Hollywood movies, where the men are dashing, like Clark Gable, and the women saints, like Norma Shearer. This is the real betrayal by Hollywood, but the actual instance of betrayal that gives the novel its title is more ironic and complex. For a period of time Hollywood quite anomalously subverted the ethic of machismo by producing a number of "women" films featuring powerful and dominating female characters like Bette Davis and Barbara Stanwyck. Toto had been dying to get his father to come to the movies with him so he could share this major portion of his life with him. But the one time he gets him to come, it is to one of these subversive "women" films, *Blood and Sand*, where the dashing male lead is betrayed and destroyed by the compelling Rita Hayworth, and the properly submissive and saintly Norma Shearer is left in the lurch. Toto does not like the film, because he has identified, as always, with the submissive female lead. But Berto shows enthusiasm about the film (which Toto takes as a final betrayal of himself by his father). Though nothing is said directly in the novel, the reader suspects that Berto has identified with the weak male lead[3] and has taken masochistic pleasure from being completely dominated by the woman, Rita Hayworth, just as, perhaps, he secretly wishes Mita would dominate him.

Puig has said that when he began writing the novel, it was to be about the loves of a cousin of his. Ultimately he made himself, as Toto, the center, but that cousin, Héctor, remains as an important and interesting character. He is the son for all the fathers to be proud of: tall, handsome, manly, a poor student (opposite to the sissy Toto), and the dedicated deflowerer of every virgin in town, the perfect product of the culture. At odd moments we glimpse in him more sensitivity than we expect, a sensitivity completely at odds with his macho role. If he had not had his role foisted on him, he might have loved someone rather than leading a life given over to endless and finally boring affairs. There is a sadness here because he has accepted his culture so completely out of innocence. He might have been happy and good; instead, during his life he will cause harm to others, and have little to show for it himself.

Almost all the characters in the novel are such, squirming inside roles they fit poorly, but Puig has put in at least one successful human being, Paquí. She is the daughter of a drunk, and perhaps her somewhat dubious situation on the perimeter of the society has given her a certain freedom. Like Mita, she is very bright and a passionate reader of novels. But she has a strong sense of independence Mita did not have. She is full of healthy sexuality and curiosity, and at fifteen she has begun doing some experimenting. But by hook or crook she maintains her virginity—essential in this society of exploitation and victimization—despite gaining a reputation for running around. She is lucky, but also honest and tough, and, perhaps because of this, instead of being taken advantage of, she seems to bring out the best in most of those she comes in contact with. In the end she marries a serious young teacher, someone she can share her intellectual life with, and someone who loves her sexually, but who also trusts her, instead of following the machismo rule (as Berto did) of violent jealousy. When Toto, jealous of Paquí's normalcy and happiness, runs to tell the teacher what a wild past she has, the teacher is angry at Toto for his spitefulness, but he says he only cares about what Paquí is now, not about her past.

Toto, at the center of the novel, is in some ways the

most harmed and the most betrayed by the false values of the society. We have seen his sexuality twisted away from him, inverted and hideously repressed. He resists learning about sex and looks the other way when his teachers try to explain it to him. Sex to him is something frightening; he conceives of having sex as being consumed by some sort of sea monster. When one of the big boys at an expensive private school Toto attends begins systematically raping all the smaller boys, most submit to the big boy's power, but Toto is so neurotically terrified and repressed that he escapes even the most ingenious traps the big boy sets for him. Toto lives entirely in the movies he goes to with his mother and lives her own aesthetic life vicariously for her when she cannot, telling her the plots to all the movies when she is in late pregnancy and can't leave the house. The sentimental romanticized beauty is what he wants, where death does not need to be believed in and where the messy parts of sex take place off camera. The misery of his real life makes him jealous and spiteful of the happiness of others, and so he spreads rumors or says nasty things to hurt people. But he is bright and sensitive, the best student in school, and if his aesthetic sense is founded on Hollywood kitsch, it is nonetheless an aesthetic sense. There is a chance he will escape his narrow oppressive surroundings to become an artist. We see hints of this in his constant daydreams about the plots of movies, revising them to include himself in them, and in his feeling that he relates to people best through the medium of telling them stories from the movies (a theme that reaches its fullest expression in *Kiss of the Spider Woman*). We see the budding artist most clearly, perhaps, in the second-to-last chapter, which is taken from the diary of Toto's piano teacher. Toto appears in this section as a character very similar to the Stephen Dedalus in the concluding sections of *Portrait of the Artist*, nervous, intellectual, opinionated, attacking the middle class, castigating God, constantly making up films and stories, and on the point of exile.

The culture of machismo and its saccharine incarnation in Hollywood is so much in the language and the lives of these people that it becomes the language and the texture of the novel itself. The popular culture enters the novel in another way as well. In the 1930s and 1940s of the novel's action, the ideas of Freudian psychoanalysis had become so widespread that they virtually became a part of the popular culture. To this day in Argentina psychoanalysis—which is falling out of favor in the United States—is very big. The novel reads at times like the transcripts from a psychoanalyst's couch. We have said that, in popular psychoanalytic terms, Toto's developing homosexuality is a classic case. The development of this homosexuality is something Puig has tried very hard to understand, and the glib "explanations" of psychoanalysis, as we follow this question over several novels, become increasingly unsatisfactory and are seen more and more as another method whereby the culture controls the individual.

*   *   *

Puig's second novel, *Heartbreak Tango*, came very much out of the same artistic impulse as the first, and the two novels, by design, complement each other.[4] By and large in *Betrayed* he had dealt with the misfits, the losers, those who had talked to him when he was a child and about whom he could write from first-hand knowledge.

But in that novel, I wasn't able to deal with the other kinds of people, the triumphant ones. . . . For me, they were really mysterious characters: the professionals, the beautiful girls who were surrounded by suitors—all those who had worked well within the system, the system of machismo, of oppression that was the only system at that time. . . . I was only able to deal with these conformist types in a literary way after my return to Argentina in 1967. I had been living abroad for ten years by then. . . . I met, quite by chance, these triumphant figures of twenty years ago who were by now all very, very disappointed with life. The system they had accepted hadn't been kind to them. . . . In Buenos Aires, I could meet them or

24

hear about what had been their fate, and knowing their point of arrival helped me to reconstruct those earlier days. (Christ, 52–53)

Now that he had his subject, he searched for the best form in which to cast it. Since language and values from the popular culture were imposed on his characters, he decided to cast his novel in a popular form, and he chose the *folletín* or serial novel. However, instead of presenting in his serial the idealized type characters coming from all walks of society, that might be found in such a novel, he had, for his cast of characters, the people who would be an audience for such novels.[5] It was a form Puig could make effective use of at the same time that he had fun with it. An actual serial, of course, would appear in monthly installments in a magazine, each episode ending in a moment of crisis or suspense to insure customers buying the next issue. Puig could not actually spread his episodes out over time,[6] but he could at least make each episode (he divided the novel not into *capítulos*, chapters, but into *entregas*, episodes) end excitingly. The other technique of the serials he could play with was the *escamoteando*, or sleight-of-hand, by which he deliberately concealed vital bits of information from the reader until the end.

Indeed, he had already played with these techniques in *Betrayed*, where, for instance, a letter Toto's father writes at the very beginning of the novel, which would have explained his virtual absence from the main part of the novel, is moved to the end, so we don't learn about it until then. The hiding of information, however, is carried out much more systematically in *Heartbreak Tango*.

Other techniques from the first novel are further developed. In addition to the letters, monologues, and unmediated dialogues of the first novel, he adds a combination of monologue and dialogue, where the characters' words are given first, followed by their real thoughts in italics (rather a cliché of popular fiction and *radionovela*). From a more sophisticated source—Puig has said he learned the freedom of mixing techniques from paging through *Ulysses*—he has added sections written in the saccharine prose of romance and sections written in the form of catechism. And in this novel for the first time appear sections in third person, although this narrative is a passionless summary description of action, free of any value judgment or subjectivity.

We quoted Puig earlier as saying that he wanted to write about reality, but he wanted the ultimate end to be beauty. Beauty, he said, came from enwrapping reality in form. The form, in the case of *Heartbreak Tango*, is the complex use he makes of the folletín. The reality it enwraps derives from Puig's childhood memories:

> Some of the characters in *Heartbreak Tango* have just one source of inspiration, one person who really existed; some are a combination; an alchemy of two or three people. All of the episodes really took place, maybe not in that order and not in the same household. But in that book, everything really happened at one time or another. (Christ, 55)

I based Juan Carlos, the protagonist, on a very vague childhood memory. There was in my village, Villegas [the village of General Villegas becomes, in Puig's first two novels, Coronel Vallejos], a boy [named Danilo] who was between twenty and thirty years old, very good looking, always very solicitous, who didn't work. The first time he came to my attention was at a ladies' tea, where he was the only man. Naturally, at five in the afternoon all the husbands, relatives, and boy friends of those present were working. He was very affectionate with me. When we got home mama rubbed me with alcohol. She explained to me that this boy was tubercular, that he had only a short time to live. It was a terrible shock, because you wouldn't suspect anything from his physical appearance. . . . In a short time, Danilo died. It was very sad because he was a gentle person with a good character, from a very well liked middle-class family, nothing to do with the Juan Carlos of the novel, who was poisoned by resentments. . . . Years later I associated Danilo with another boy, also unemployed, not through sickness, but through lack of skills, which in that time was called vagrancy. They were very similar physically. This one was bad humored and resentful, from a family that came to nothing. He was an implacable Don Juan. In writing the novel I fused both characters into one; from Danilo all I took was his extraordinary physical appearance and his sickness. All the defects are from the other. As for the other characters . . . Mabel is based on a single model. (Monegal, 26)

Though the novel is perfectly serious, it is, in a way characterstic of Puig, based in part on a two-sided joke. On one side is that hoariest cliché of dirty jokes that people dying of tuberculosis are always oversexed, while on the other side is the romantic cliché of the beautiful Camille-like heroine dying glamorously of consumption.

Juan Carlos is at the center of the novel, with all other characters rayed about him like the spokes of a wheel, all their movements depending on his. Puig has said that when he conceived his first novel, Héctor, the boy shaped in the image of machismo, was to be the central character, and only as the novel developed did he become secondary to Toto, who was in effect a sort of mirror image of him, showing the two ways that basically good, innocent boys are damaged by the prevailing culture. In the second novel Puig has put the macho figure at the center. It is a character fascinating to Puig, which will recur in various forms in most of his novels. But if in the other novels this figure has redeeming qualities and clearly seems as much victim as victimizer, in *Heartbreak* the character appears to be absolutely harmful.

He seems to be a naturalistic character, almost clinically presented. And yet I don't think it is too much to say he is an archetype, both representative and symbolical embodiment of the popular culture. As such he becomes virtually the mythopoeic center of Puig's writing. If indeed he embodies the machismo-centered culture—he is literally named Don Juan—then it is significant that Puig casts him as diseased, that he casts him as unable to mature, as perpetually to the day of his death a spoiled adolescent, his mother and sister sacrificing their lives to him and receiving nothing in return but bitterness and loneliness. Nelida, his girl friend, devotes her life to her memory of him. She received nothing from him, not even sex, and the memory of him poisons the happiness she might have had. When she can't have Juan Carlos she marries someone else for convenience, despises him, and ignores the children she has by him. Only when she is dying of cancer in her early fifties does she suddenly, too late, realize that her husband was a good man who loved her and that she has fine children. Juan Carlos's sister has mistakenly assumed that Nelida was responsible for Juan Carlos's death, and she devotes her whole life to a meaningless vendetta against her. A widow who was a *pis aller* for Juan Carlos bankrupts herself supporting Juan Carlos, who, at his death, leaves her with nothing. Everyone who comes in contact with him is infected, not by his tuberculosis but by his system of values. On the next social level down, Pancho, the half-breed, might have married Fanny, the servant, and had good strong children, a happy married life, and a good job in the police force, except that Juan Carlos had infused the ideas of machismo in him. He should not marry her, but seduce and abandon her, and chase after other women, with the result that Fanny, who has also imbibed from the poisonous culture, knows that according to the rules she must murder him.

If it seems strange that such allegiance should be paid to Juan Carlos, Puig says we must appreciate how drab life was in the little town on the remote flat barren stretches of the pampas, as far removed from the mountains as from the sea, with the culture of the city only a distant rumor. People needed to have some object on which to project their dreams of beauty, and Juan Carlos was all they could find. "Since he had a perfect face, he invited them to judge he also had a perfect soul."[7]

What runs through the novel, in epigraphs to the different episodes, in the daydreams of the characters, are the words from the tangos and boleros popular at that time.[8] These words give the characters clues on how to act and teach them that in every event they must react with grand passion. At the lowest social level the innocents like Pancho and Fanny accept it completely. Pancho abandons her and chases after another woman because that is what a passionate, red-blooded man does. Never mind the fact that the other woman is really not very good looking with her heavy hips and skinny legs, never mind the fact that he would prefer to spend time with his wonderful son. When he climbs down out of the window from his assignation with the other woman, Fanny knows, because she has heard it in the songs, that she must be waiting for him with the butcher knife in her hands.

Above that level of innocence, in the middle class from which most of the characters come, we see the lie. The words from the songs give a vocabulary of passion, but behind the vocabulary is calculation and shrewd and passionless maneuvering. Nelida, for example, was seduced by her boss at an early age, but she has covered this up. She is sexually attracted to Juan Carlos, but instead of submitting to him as the passionate songs would suggest, she coyly fends him off and pretends to be a virgin, because she hopes he will marry her. For his part, he is not even interested in her; he is using her as a blind to account for how he spends his evenings, because after he leaves her each night, he climbs into Mabel's bedroom window, the rich girl, and they make love until the small hours. Mabel is the biggest lie of all, because, rather than being the respectable but ultimately submissive victimized female, she is the most rapaciously and aggressively sexual of all the characters, damaging Juan Carlos's health with her all-night demands and when he is dead inviting Pancho up to her room, because any young man will do.

In keeping with a nineteenth-century serial novel, the last chapter is an account of what happened to the characters in the future. Juan Carlos's sister (this is twenty years after his death) puts a new plaque on his tomb, never having been able to forget him. Pancho's son, Panchito, has married a good housewife and has a good job as a mechanic—Pancho, however, his skeleton lying in a common grave, does not see this. Nelida, before dying, is able to tell her husband she loves him and has forgotten Juan Carlos, and her husband is pleased and grateful—

but obviously they have lost their whole married life together. Mabel is struggling to get money to send her two-year-old grandson, who is crippled with polio, to specialists. This last account almost seems like a bit of revengeful meanness on the part of Puig himself, except that perhaps the polio, like the tuberculosis and Nelida's cancer, is part of the disease imagery throughout the novel, depicting in this case the crippling infection of the culture that can be carried through a life and visited on succeeding generations. This novel of the successful ones, of those who play by the rules, is surely Puig's blackest. It is the only one of his novels in which no one is saved.

*   *   *

Puig's first two novels recaptured for him the 1940s and the 1950s in his small town of Coronel Vallejos. With them he felt he had said everything he had to say about life on the pampas at that period. In his next novel, *The Buenos Aires Affair* (1973), Puig took his story to the big city, Buenos Aires, and set it in the present. In the big city, Marta Morello-Frosch points out, "It is important to note that the characters of this last novel don't have a narrow horizon, don't live in a tiny provincial town, have access to culture, travel, can even move in artistic circles, have, up to a point, the ingredients of the ideal dreams, and are not constrained by provincial mentalities."[9] But under the surface, nothing in the society has changed. And so this novel marks not a change but a progression. In *Betrayed*, the characters are presented to us in dialogue and in interior monologue. In *Heartbreak Tango*, the characters live so much on the surface of the culture and so completely out of touch with themselves that there is very little interior monologue. In *The Buenos Aires Affair* the characters live so completely within their dreams that there is virtually no dialogue.[10]

Puig continued using his shifting kaleidoscope of

narrative styles and filtering the perceptions of his characters through the popular culture that gave them their vocabulary. And once more he tried the experiment of casting the novel itself in a popular subliterary form, in this case, as the subtitle indicates, as a detective story.

According to Juan Armando Epple, the structure of a detective story or mystery thriller is rigidly determined. First of all, there is the primacy of the event—the crime that must be solved. Then, there are two opposed points of view, one provided by the narrator, who knows everything and uses trickery to hide facts, only dosing them out slowly over the course of the novel; and the other provided by the reader, who, seizing on these clues, uses ordinary logic to work them out, hoping to do it faster than the author lets him. The original act seems to go against the rules of reality—for example, all the doors to the room where the murder has taken place are locked—but in the end is found to conform to them. Reality itself—the normal world—is not questioned. The reader's approach is intellectual. The normal law-abiding world is reaffirmed at the end. So, in the beginning is the crime; in the middle is the investigation; in the end the truth is discovered and the guilty are punished. There is a dramatic structure, beginning with a mystery that needs unraveling. The characters merely serve this structure; they are uncomplicated: a criminal, a victim, an investigator, and so on.[11]

It is the structure Puig has in mind, and in a superficial way his novel at least in the beginning seems to follow it. For example, *Affair* indeed begins with a mystery. A woman awakes to find that her thirty-five-year-old daughter has vanished. In the next scene we see the daughter bound and gagged, nude, on a bed, and a muscular man with only a towel wrapped around him is approaching threateningly. But before the actual violation is committed, we back up in time and are given a quick summary of the daughter's life, couched in terms of popular psychology. Then we hear about a mysterious phone call to the police saying an unbalanced man is about to commit a violent crime. Then we back up in time again and get a quick summary of the life of the man who is holding the daughter captive, once more in terms of pop Freudian psychology. So far, in *structure*, the novel is holding closely to the popular subliterary genre of the mystery thriller.

Puig says the mystery is a form he loves. Nevertheless at each point what is interesting about his novel is the way in which it differs from the subliterary form. Indeed, the contrast between the implied form and Puig's real form helps him to make his thematic statements. Let me examine some of the differences.

Puig's first two novels received considerable critical attention. He is known to his audience as a serious writer, so when he puts as a subtitle to his novel "*Novela Policial,*" no reader is naive enough to expect a simple thriller. The reader is alerted to watch in what way Puig will play with the form. Although Puig has repeatedly denied parodic intent, the writing at the beginning is obviously parodic of police report prose: "A pale winter sun lighted the place in question." The narrative includes an overstated cheap ploy to create a sense of foreboding: "During that moment in which she closed her eyes someone could have entered the room without her noticing him" (*BAA,* 4, 6). Although in part Puig may intend to create a sense of foreboding and suspense, clearly his chief intention in these opening pages is to be comic and to signal to us that he is playing with the form he has adopted.

The second scene, in which the man stands threateningly before the bound, drugged, nude woman, is so extreme in its style it seems scarcely intended to achieve a dramatic effect. It is written in prose reminiscent of the nouveau roman, with a painstakingly detailed description of the apartment in which the threatening man and bound woman are given no more importance, no more emotional weight, than the other objects in the room. It is also perhaps a parody—and no other word will serve—of the careful description of the scene of the crime from which we are to gather clues as to who did what. Significantly (I will explain why shortly), in this case, the violent crime does not yet seem to have been committed.

These distancing mechanisms signal to us that the mystery story form is being manipulated in a very sophisticated way and for purposes beyond those usually expected from the genre. Other mechanisms distancing the reader include the epigraphs from Hollywood movies heading each section and the dazzling array of narrative styles and effects (compared to the generally slovenly prose of the genre itself).

But even with all this stated, it must be admitted that in some respects Puig has his cake and eats it too. The more overtly parodic elements occur mainly at the beginning of the novel, as if perhaps Puig felt it necessary to authenticate his legitimate literary uses of his popular form. But then an odd thing happens. A sense of foreboding *is* created. We *do* examine the apartment closely for clues. And especially in reading the sociological report of the characters' lives, we follow their careers avidly, we are convinced by the psychological explanations for their behavior (though recognizing, as the novel progresses, how little they really seem to explain). Once more, the characters somehow seem all the more real to us by being presented in such an apparently artless form—as if once again we are getting unsorted information that we must ourselves put together into a coherent pattern. So in fact, just as Puig claimed it would, the form, or the apparent form, of the mystery thriller is working on us successfully. When it pleases Puig, he is distancing himself from the form, but also when it pleases him, he is making use of it to achieve his effects.

But mainly he is violating the form at every turn for thematic reasons. First of all, the "crime" is never committed—he is stopped before he can carry it out. And second, it would not have been a crime. In fact, the crime was the prevention of the man's actions. In the world of the detective novel, the forces of society prevent or punish crimes against citizens of that society. In Puig's world it is precisely opposite, as the forces of society commit crimes against citizens and prevent them from working out their own salvation.

I have suggested that a part of Puig's fun in writing *Heartbreak Tango* was treating seriously certain jokes or clichés about tuberculosis. A similar double-pronged cliché and joke is at the thematic heart of *Affair*. If dying glamorously of consumption is a cliché of romantic fiction, certainly the hoariest cliché of mystery-thriller fiction is the innocent heroine under threat of being tortured and ravished ("under threat of death . . . or worse," as Mrs. Radcliffe used to put it) by the diabolical villain. The joke—in the pornographic version—is that the heroine really enjoys it. There is also the joke that a sadist and a masochist together form a pair able to satisfy each other perfectly.[12]

It is these popular jokes that Puig treats quite seriously in his novel. Leo is a reductio ad absurdum of the male brought up in the machismo culture: the culture has molded him into a permanently immature sadist, with any decent impulses in his being so repressed that he can relate to another person only through sexual violence. In this sense he is a more extreme version of Héctor in *Betrayed* and Juan Carlos in *Heartbreak Tango*. Gladys, on her side, is brought up to be so repressed and submissive that she can only be fulfilled through being violently victimized. What else, at heart—Puig seems to ask— is the system of macho men and submissive women? In real life many people act out their roles dishonestly and use their roles calculatingly for self gain. But Leo and Gladys are the pure and innocent Adam and Eve of machismo, so created by their society that they give full and honest expression to its values. What is significant, despite their neurosis bordering on and occasionally crossing into psychosis, is that because of their honesty there is actually a chance—even though they must express their relationship through the sick terms of their culture—that they will be able to come together and relate to each other as human beings. But here is the one thing, Puig seems to say, the society will not allow. All the other characters, however well meaning on the surface, combine to cheat them of their fulfillment together.

34

Thus, as stated earlier, the crime novel form is subverted. Rather than Leo committing a crime against society, society commits a crime against Leo. A further signal that form is being subverted is that the death of the criminal at the end is always an unimportant event in human terms—merely the appropriate last step in the working out of the form. In *Affair,* on the contrary, rather than simply forgetting about Leo as soon as he is dead, in chapter fourteen we have one of the most extraordinary passages in all of Puig's writing. Puig describes in precise sickening detail each stage in the decomposition of Leo's body, and at each moment we must contrast the rotting carcass with the living man, who had such wonderful physical and intellectual attributes that he was able to achieve a great deal despite the damage his society had done to him.

Gladys is an artist of great power, and Leo an influential art critic. No doubt Puig has concealed another joke here (the artist as masochist, the critic as sadist) and has more seriously pursued the theme that the artist needs his critic (intelligent audience) just as the audience needs its artists. We know that Puig takes these ideas seriously, because just as Toto in *Betrayed* was meant to represent Puig himself as a little boy, so, it seems obvious, is Gladys intended as an adult version of him. Her career parallels Puig's closely, as do her artistic methods.

The parallels in their lives are worth examining. Puig was born in 1932; Gladys was born in 1934. In 1956, when he was twenty-four, Puig won a scholarship to study abroad (in Italy); in 1959, when she was twenty-four, Gladys won a scholarship to study abroad (in the United States). Like young Puig, Gladys seems to see the world in terms of Hollywood movies. Puig returned to Argentina in 1967; Gladys returns in 1968. She has been lonely, uncertain of what direction to take in her art, and she is on the verge of a nervous breakdown. Puig was lonely and miserable, and he counted himself a failure. But before returning he discovered the true direction his art was to take. Gladys does not discover the direction of her own art until she returns. But when she does discover her technique of *bricolage*, it is exactly Puig's technique for writing his novels (see Chapter 1).

It has been necessary to point out these parallels to demonstrate that Puig has intended her to represent a genuine artist. Leo at first recognizes her talent and awards her a major national prize, but later, neurotically rejecting her, he takes the prize away from her and gives it to another woman. Some commentators on the novel appear to have taken Leo's second judgment as the true one, so that, for example, Robert Alter can speak of her as "a painter of uncertain talents."[13] But I think we are meant to see the second woman Leo gives the prize to as conventional and mediocre (she, after all, as a representative of the society, is the one who is instrumental in denying Leo and Gladys their moment of fulfillment). Leo, separated from Gladys's true and perhaps saving art, at last is overcome by guilt at the violence of his past actions and kills himself.

Gladys, properly to her submissive role, is overcome by a sense of low worth (taking Leo's second valuation of her art as the true one) and is herself on the point of suicide. But at this darkest moment salvation comes to her. Through the thin walls of the apartment she has heard the sounds of normal loving sex from the couple next door. When the husband goes to work, the young wife calls her to come over. The young wife, wondering to herself if her husband has just planted the seed of new life in her, gives Gladys milk to drink and, seeing that she is exhausted, puts her to bed. These are symbolic acts of motherhood, and the seed of new life in her is Gladys's rebirth through an act of love that is neither exploitation nor victimization. Others recognizing Gladys's talent and going against Leo's second judgment, arrange for an exhibition of her work. We feel Gladys will pursue this opening for her new career.

III. SAVED BY
HEDY LAMARR

What helped me mainly were all the liberation movements that have taken place lately, in Argentina as well as [in the United States]. The women's liberation movement is one of the most important things that ever happened.

Manuel Puig, interviewed by Ronald Christ

IN his previous novels, Puig's characters have been imprisoned by their culture in a world so bleak and gray and with so few options that they have turned to the spurious glamor of Hollywood movies in order to have some beauty in their lives. Clearly, then, the setting of *Kiss of the Spider Woman* (1976) provides the perfect and inevitable objective correlative for his themes: virtually the entirety of the novel takes place inside a prison cell in Buenos Aires, where the two characters are locked in together with nothing to do but discuss Hollywood movies in order to pass the time away. It is no wonder if, at times, the movies take on for them the guise of reality while their own lives are reduced to "a class Z movie" in which they are stuck by mistake.

Having found his perfect objective correlative, Puig seems also to have found his perfect form, for almost all of this novel comes to us in the form of unmediated dialogue between the two cellmates, so that nearly the entire action of the novel is transmitted to us through the two voices speaking.[1]

The characters in this novel are perfected versions of characters we have seen in the earlier novels. Puig has maintained that in the culture of machismo, men are molded into sadistic oppressors of the weak, especially of women, whom the society forces into the mold of submissive sex objects. For the man who rejects the stereotypical male role, there is only one option, a complete

37

inversion of sexuality—an acceptance of the only other role model offered, that of a submissive woman. In *Betrayed by Rita Hayworth*, we saw Toto, too sensitive and timid for the macho role, sliding into homosexuality. This is the case of one of the cellmates, Molina, a thirty-seven-year-old homosexual imprisoned for corrupting the morals of minors. The previous novel, *The Buenos Aires Affair*, had hinted that there might after all be another option. Leo had flirted briefly with becoming an anti-government leftist as a way in which he could channel his aggressiveness toward helping rather than harming others. But the police, the custodians of the macho society, captured and tortured him, and re-molded him into the society's image. In *Kiss of the Spider Woman* the other cellmate, Valentin, a twenty-six-year-old leftist—more than a leftist, a committed *guerrillero*—has been imprisoned for subversive activities. He represents, in Puig's novels, a new option for men, a positive way to reject the authority of oppressors. He is able to remain male and yet to fight against male oppression and champion women's rights. Puig had often suggested that in many of his Don Juan figures there was a certain sensitivity and human decency that wanted expression but that was always thwarted. Marxism, he seems to say, is a possible channel.

The female characters in Puig, the submissive masochistic side of the machismo equation, have also been, heretofore, presented as having two options: either to be the submissive victims of male dominance or to pretend submission while making calculated use of the system to gain their own ends. Inside his female characters, pushed to one or other of these unsatisfactory extremes, Puig has hinted that there is sometimes a sensitive and decent human being concealed, an individual who would like to give and receive love, and at the same time preserve human dignity. By a nice economy of means, in *Kiss of the Spider Woman* Molina represents not only the male's homosexual option but also the role of the oppressed woman who, as Barbara Mujica points out, is at one and the same time an "able manipulator" with even the prison warden doing his bidding.[2] Since Valentin's name suggests the stereotypical macho hero Valentino, the two characters, Molina and Valentin, represent within themselves all the major character types from Puig's previous fictions.

These characters, once more, have no language to speak, cannot even think their deepest thoughts, except with the vocabulary of the popular culture, the only vocabulary given to them. Molina sees the world in terms of Hollywood clichés that in effect block him from seeing the world. Valentin on his side sees the world screened through popular Freudian psychology and the clichés of a Marxism he barely understands.

In the grim eventless tedium of prison life, the movies lovingly remembered by Molina become for the two inmates—and for the reader as well—the text of reality.[3]

> "I'm sorry it's over [Valentin says] . . . because I've become attached to the characters. And now it's over, and it's just like they died."[4]

Since the movies come to represent reality to the characters, a report from the world "out there," Valentin wants them to be remembered and told accurately, and he is irritated when he thinks Molina is changing things to make a better story.

> "Then you're inventing half the picture."
> "No, I'm not inventing, I swear, but some things, to round them out for you, so you can see them the way I'm seeing them . . . well, to some extent I have to embroider a little." (KSW, 18)

The parallel with what Puig does in writing a novel is obvious at every point: giving a report on reality filtered through the popular culture but embroidered a little so we can see it the way he does. Molina even favors a folletín style. When he is about to leave off telling the movie for the night (literally at the end of one of Puig's chapters), Valentin says:

"Go on a little bit more."

"A little bit, no more, I like to leave you hanging, that way you enjoy the film more. You have to do it that way with the public, otherwise they're not satisfied. On the radio they always used to do that to you. And now on the TV soaps." (*KSW*, 25–26)

A problem is that the parts of the movies seeming important to Molina—what they are wearing, the hair styles, the furnishings—are not important to Valentin, who insists, "Don't waste so much time, tell me what happens" (*KSW*, 50). Furthermore, Valentin is not always satisfied with Molina's interpretations of "reality"—he wants to impose his own meanings. Molina wants beauty and suspense; Valentin wants his reductive psychological truth.

"She really is a panther woman."
"No, she's a psychopathic killer." (*KSW*, 39)

It is through experiencing the movies together and expressing their different reactions to them that the two characters come to know each other and learn to respect each other's value systems, each moving toward the other's position. But at least initially, their social philosophies are opposed.

"Live for the moment! Enjoy life a little! . . ."
"I don't believe in that business of living for the moment . . . my life is dedicated to political struggle . . . . I can put up with everything in here . . . because there's a purpose behind it. Social revolution." (*KSW*, 27)

Throughout his life Molina has mortgaged his future for the sake of present pleasure. This indeed is why he is in prison. Valentin, on the other hand, has given up all present pleasure for the sake of a future he probably will not live to see. Both are extreme positions. Valentin's leads him to reduce other human beings to an abstract value.

"My ideals . . . that's my real strength."
"And your girl?"
"That's . . . secondary." (*KSW*, 28)

But if Valentin sees things only abstractly, Molina sees them only personally, and this has led him into betrayal. We learn as the novel progresses that Molina has been planted in the cell to ferret information about the guerrillas out of Valentin. The leverage the prison warden has is the illness of Molina's mother; if Molina cooperates they have promised to let him out to take care of her.

The prison officials systematically poison Valentin's food to weaken his spirit and make it easier for Molina to break down his suspiciousness. The poisoning indeed brings Valentin to a low ebb, but what it destroys is not his suspiciousness—he never had much—but his abstractions. Instead of seeing himself and Molina as merely counters of "secondary" importance on the road to the future, he sees them now as human beings: if in abstract theory all human beings are equal, then that means in real life men and women both are equal, and if they are equal that means they do not have different roles to play in the world, they have the same role, and therefore they can love each other equally, not just macho men and submissive women but everyone equally, including members of the same sex sharing physical love. His abstract clichés have brought him to a very human conclusion. The two men consummate their love in the cell, and they are perhaps the best, the most honest, and the most gentle lovers to appear in Puig's fiction.

I have said that virtually all of the novel is given to us in the form of dialogue between Molina and Valentin. But, as we have come to expect from Puig, there are at least a few other narrative styles. About sixty pages into the novel, footnotes begin to appear at the bottom of the page and continue, intermittently, for the greater part of the rest of the novel. The first concerns one of the movies Molina narrates. The second, and longest, is a carefully researched essay on various theories of the origin of homosexuality. The essay tries to give scholarly backing to the conclusion of the two cellmates. It goes through every theory of the origin of homosexuality: physical predisposition, homosexual seduction at an early impressionable age, oedipal fixation, and so on, rejecting each in turn, until it reaches the argument by Brown and Marcuse that man is by nature polymorphous-perverse, but that society for its own needs of procreation forces human beings —within the framework of machismo—into the unnatural exclusivity of heterosexual roles in order to serve its own ends. The love between Valentin and Molina, we may conclude, is neither immoral nor unnatural; it is an expression of nature itself that the society is seeking to crush.[5]

> When I wrote *Rita Hayworth*, I still believed in Clark Gable as a force of Nature. I thought it was a cruel Nature that had made this strong man and these weak Harlows but that it was, in fact, Nature's law. Now I am convinced that Clark Gable is an historical-cultural product, not Nature's creature. (Christ, 61)

Society has its subjects within its power (symbolized in the novel by the characters being in a prison cell), and it punishes deviation from its rules savagely. What is most unforgivable to a society based on domination and submission, it would seem, is love between one human being and another. At the end of the novel Valentin has been brutally tortured and is perhaps near death. Molina has been released in the hope that he will lead the police to the Guerrillas. He does in fact attempt to carry them a message from Valentin. When they are too suspicious to come to a rendezvous, the police step in to rearrest Molina, at which point the guerrillas kill him so he cannot be interrogated.

Superficially, there appears to be a victory for authority: the two rebels against machismo are destroyed. But if we look closely, that has not been the case at all. Valentin, we have already seen, has come an enormous distance from his macho upbringing. He has also come closer to

Molina's position in focusing on the present moment of life.

> "It's a question [he now says] of learning to accept things as they come, and to appreciate the good that happens to you, even if it doesn't last. Because nothing is forever." (*KSW*, 259)

But Molina, in his way, has moved just as far toward Valentin's position. Though objecting that he is not cast in the heroic mold, he agrees to try to carry the message for Valentin. He does this to be worthy of his love. When he gets out of prison, he rejects his waiter boyfriend—a Don Juan type who had exploited him—and, spending a certain amount of time each day sitting by a window facing toward the prison, shows his fidelity to Valentin. So far, of course, he is still really living within the ideals of the boleros and Hollywood movies. As bourgeois female he has always said his dream was to have a real man he could be faithful to all his life, and Valentin has become that man. And now, as movie heroine, he wants to go and sacrifice his life for him. As Alicia Borinsky points out, Molina has become the "star" of the novel.[6] But in a way the peak of his life comes in a small moment overlooked by everyone else involved. Seconds before the guerrillas streak by and shoot him, the police come up to him to take him back into custody—*and he asks to see their credentials* (*KSW*, 274). That tiny action says he no longer regards himself as inherently inferior, inherently, by act of nature, a victim. In that moment he stands up for his rights, and it is as a direct result of his teaching by Valentin. At nearly that same moment, perhaps, Valentin, given morphine by a compassionate doctor, has gone into a rapturous dream, not of abstract love for the future but of personal love in the present— something Molina had taught him not to be ashamed of.

It is the synthesis of their partial views that has in the end made them complete human beings. And once more, the synthesis has had to be effected through the clichés of popular culture, since they had no other vocabulary with which to formulate it. Once more the marvel is their human capacity to twist the shoddy clichés into significant expression.

There is a handsome fitting of pattern into pattern. Puig takes the vulgar materials of the popular culture and creates out of them meaningful fictions for his readers. Within the novel is the same transaction. Molina as artist shapes the materials of his culture to create significance for Valentin as audience. It is *The Buenos Aires Affair* once more, artist and critic, but working out more positively this time: in his final dream Valentin has taken the materials given him by Molina and, artist-*bricoleur* himself, refashioned them into life-changing, life-salvaging meaning of his own.

*　　*　　*

During the course of the novel *Kiss of the Spider Woman*, Molina narrates the plots of several movies, and he and Valentin identify more and more closely with the characters, and the plots touch their lives more and more directly, until they are virtually acting out the movies themselves. The last movie Molina tells is about a remarkably beautiful actress and singer kept by a powerful magnate. A young journalist in love with her helps her avoid a scandal (at an early stage in her career she had posed in the nude) and asks her to run off with him. When she won't, he quits his job, drops out of life, and becomes a drunk. She leaves her keeper, but he is so powerful he can stop her from resuming her career. She comes to help the dying journalist but can only get money to feed him by becoming a prostitute.[7]

This unlikely but supremely romantic story has its basis in fact—at the beginning of the story, if not at the ending. The movie is based on the life of no less famous a beauty and actress than Hedy Lamarr. Hedy Lamarr was born in Vienna in 1913 and gained worldwide fame and notoriety when she appeared nude in a Czech film in 1933. Shortly after, she married an Austrian munitions magnate who tried to have every print of that film destroyed and to end her movie career. But she divorced him and made sure the film continued to circulate. She came to Hollywood in 1938, billed as the most beautiful woman in the world, but she turned out to be a mediocre actress. She played a "woman of mystery" several times. In 1965 she was arrested on a shoplifting charge.[8]

The reader who finishes *Kiss of the Spider Woman* and immediately begins reading Puig's next novel, *Pubis Angelical* (1979), may think he is listening to one of Molina's narratives, for here is the Hedy Lamarr story again, told to us in a lush, romanticized third-person narrative. It is the mid–1930s. We see the woman, whose appearance and situation exactly duplicate Hedy Lamarr's, in her honeymoon house, isolated on an island in the Black Sea, with guards all around her. The furnishings are those Molina described, down to the ermine rugs. When she awakes, the night after her wedding, she has a note from her husband, the Austrian munitions magnate. He had drugged her the night before, he blandly explains, so that he could enjoy her body without having to respond to her as a person. It is the ultimate in masculine exploitation. She tries to escape, but each escape puts her into the hands of another masculine exploiter. She finally ends up in Hollywood, a purveyor of others' dreams but trapped in a contract that makes her a virtual slave.

Later in the novel this story is transposed into the future (the romantic adventure story now given sci-fi trappings, as another ingredient of the popular culture). In the first story the woman, in keeping with her role as simply an exploited body, has no personal name but is known only as "the Mistress." In the future narrative the woman's role is spelled out even more starkly. Also nameless, she simply has a designation, W218. Instead of being exploited by a series of men, she is directly exploited by the state. She is performing her national service as a sex partner to elderly men, a direct physical purveyor of their fantasies. In her attempts to escape, she similarly goes from one exploiter to the next.

Sandwiched between these two narratives is the realistic story of Ana in time-present. The two stories are evidently dreams deep in Ana's unconscious as she waits in a hospital in Mexico for the outcome of her cancer operations.

Ana is presented to us through Puig's more typical narrative form of unmediated dialogues, which she is engaged in with her friend Beatrice and with her ex-boyfriend Pozzi. We also see her diary entries. She is revealed to us as a standard Argentine bourgeoise, very close in her tastes and beliefs to Molina. Her life's dream, in fact, is identical to Molina's: "The only thing that gives me the desire to go on living . . . is to think that some day I will meet a man who is worthwhile."[9] Having gone from one exploiter to the next, she finds that her life has not been very promising so far. She is in Mexico to get away from a suitor in her native Argentina who is high up in the dictatorship and pursuing her with a mixture of threats and gifts. Sharing her exile is her ex-boyfriend Pozzi, who, though a leftist guerrilla full of liberal ideas, also seems to think of her in terms of exploitation. He wants her to lure her powerful suitor to Mexico, where he can be kidnapped for exchange with leftist prisoners. The situation is similar to that of Valentin wanting Molina to carry messages for him. Indeed the relationship between Ana and Pozzi parallels at every important point the relationship between Molina and Valentin. In each case is the same ambiguity: is sacrifice of the self for others always a form of exploitation, or can it sometimes lead to self fulfillment? Pozzi's final argument to her is that she knows she is dying of cancer anyway, and so she ought to do something worthwhile with her life (he means luring her fascist suitor into a trap). She had not been facing the possibility of her death, and his brutality in bringing it out makes her refuse him definitively (the opposite conclusion to *Kiss of the Spider Woman*, where Molina accepts). Pozzi's brutality is proof to her that he is only using her. But as evidence that he seriously believes sacrifice for others is worthwhile, he returns to Argentina to help in the cause against the dictators and is at once killed. She continues to wonder, "Whose death will have . . . more meaning? . . . mine . . . or his?" (*PA*, 213).

The future narrative is left in the same ambiguity. At the end W218 volunteers herself as sex partner for those in the contagious hospital, where she is greatly beloved, and is quickly infected with a terminal disease. Lying on her deathbed she listens to the story of the crazy woman on the bed next to her, about her daughter's "pubis angelical." The men are killing each other in civil war, but when the girl appears among them and raises her skirt, she reveals the statue-like pubis of an angel: without hair or genitalia. The men, struck dumb, stop fighting. If all fighting is for dominance, and if the desire to dominate grows out of that first desire of men to have control over women's bodies, then perhaps peace can come only if women make a radical denial of their sex, creating a new *Lysistrata*. Marta Morello-Frosch says that at the end of the novel "happiness finally is identified with an *absence of desire*, with a lack of sex, with the pubis angelical."[10] Gustavo Pellón points out the problem with that conclusion: "But the fable itself contains the seeds of its own failure, since the best it can offer is an end to exploitation when the object of exploitation itself ceases to exist" (Pellón, 199).

Perhaps Puig means not to resolve the dilemma finally but only provisionally. For now, at least, Ana has another priority. The three women, "The Mistress," Ana, and W218, dividing the century among them, all with parallel experiences, all look exactly like Hedy Lamarr. "The Mistress" and W218 are Ana's spiritual mother and daughter. Throughout the work, the three generations have been desperately trying to contact each other. Ana had been estranged from her real mother, and she was allowing her real daughter to be raised by her odious former husband. At the end of the novel, a final cancer operation has been successful. Ana is cured and has a new chance at life. At least for the time being, she is sexually numb, and finding a new masculine protector does not enter into her plans. What she wants now is to reestablish contact with her mother and her daughter. It is a hopeful ending. Women should not allow themselves to be raised with the values of the male-dominated culture that tells women they are weak things to be owned by the males. The generations of women must come together and teach each other, learn from each other's experiences.

How did Ana arrive at her conclusion? Both deliberately and unconsciously she has been sifting through the only kinds of evidence available to her, the Hollywood/sci-fi narratives of her dreams, Pozzi's trendy Lacan and Marx, her friend Beatrice's feminism. It is once more a triumphant reshaping of the usually treacherous materials of the popular culture.

* * *

After his first two years of exile in Mexico, Puig spent the next two years, 1976 through 1978, in New York. It was not a happy time for Puig.

I arrived in the United States—where I had lived in January of 1976—without papers, without an apartment, a few years older and in a New York less welcoming than before. A country that had left the hippie euphoria (a very important attempt at liberation that failed in the end), I arrived at a defeated city which thus summed up my personal problems. So that 1976 was a horrible, black year. I had then a very violent clash with a fascinating North American. It was a problem lived in English and I wanted to write about it. I asked permission of this person to take notes over his life: I took some two hundred pages of notes in English. . . . The North American is a young man of the left who rejects the whole system in which he is immersed. (Corbatta, 619–20)

There was a neighbor of mine in the Village where I was living . . . and in some ways it occurred to me that I would like to be him. It was a special moment in my life. I had had problems with my health, I was defining the Argentine question as very bad, as something that would last a long time, in 1976 with the advent of the Junta . . . I was really tired by the language, the having to express myself in English, I had studied English many years, I had lived here in the United States and in London, but English is diabolical, you never finish learning it, I didn't feel I had mastered it, it was a sensation of impotence with the language, at the same time I admired it because it's a fantastic language. What happened is, as a medical prescription I had to go swimming every day at a gym and saw there [this neighbor] who was younger, who had terrific health and was American, that is, a master of the English language. How can some people have everything? One day we began to talk and it turned out he hated being North American, hated English, and wanted to be a writer. He wanted to be me. (Roffé, pp. 141–42)

The novel that emerged from this confrontation, *Eternal Curse on the Reader of These Pages* (1980), was in fact first written by Puig in English, though it was first published in Spanish in his translation. The story of the novel is quickly recounted: a civil-rights group gets an old man out of prison in Argentina and brings him to New York. His health is poor and he is badly shocked psychologically, to the point where he has total amnesia. He is kept in a nursing home, and a young man is employed to push him around in a wheel chair. The novel consists of the conversations between them, some actual, some imagined or hallucinated by the old man. The young American is a professor of history, a Marxist, who has dropped out of his society and now lives alone, only accepting menial jobs. The old man, also a scholar, was a subversive union organizer in Argentina. He might have been able to endure his imprisonment, but what has broken him is the murder of his wife and son by the police. His feeling of guilt that his actions are responsible for their deaths has caused him to repress his entire past, and this denial of his whole life is rapidly killing him. While he was in prison he kept notebooks in code, in which he wrote about his life. The young man looks at the notebooks and immediately sees through the code and begins translating them. They are important and he will be able to edit and publish them, making a name for himself and getting back into university teaching. At first the old man is supportive, but when the decoding begins to dig up the repressed material, the old man flares up in temper and takes the books away from him. Shortly afterward the old man dies.

The novel resembles in form *Kiss of the Spider Woman*: the story is transmitted to us almost entirely through unmediated dialogue. Virtually no other characters appear on stage. Both characters—the drop-out professor and the exiled dying old man—are essentially cut off from the rest of society. Yet despite the marginal appearance of their position in society, both are, as are the characters of *Kiss of the Spider Woman*, somehow "emblematic" of it. Just as Valentin tended to be too abstract and Molina too personal (as was also the case with Pozzi and Ana), Ramirez and Larry in this novel also tend to have partial views, which makes them feel a lack of completeness. They must come together for wholeness; in this case, the attempt is to come together not as lovers but as father and son. In this respect, the novel resembles *Pubis Angelical*, where it is necessary for the different generations—grandmother, mother, daughter—to get together to learn from each other and to consolidate their gains.

In appearance, *Eternal Curse* is the simplest of Puig's novels. It is true that the reader must pay attention to see if a given section records an actual or a fantasized conversation, nevertheless the narrative is straightforward and chronological. On the surface it would seem to be the most socially or politically oriented of Puig's novels: the old man destroyed by the cruelly repressive Argentine government, the young man more subtly damaged by the post-Vietnam materialism of American society. And yet, oddly, none of that really seems to be at issue in the novel, which is instead very personal and ambiguous. It is a novel about concealment and unmasking, each character concealing his past from the other and from himself, each trying to force the other to unmask. Perhaps it is a novel in which the "problem" Puig is working out has to do with

50

his own concealments, especially since he goes out of his way to deny that he appears in the novel.

> In this novel I am not interested in myself as a character, since the counterpart of the North American is my father. . . . In the novel, my father arrives as exile in New York . . . and this young man pushes him in his wheelchair. The English of my father is faulty, the other's is not, it's from the notes. (Corbatta, 620)

The last statement, on the language, needs to be read on several levels. At the most obvious level, Puig means that, as an Hispanic writer writing in English, he did not need to worry if the English he invented for the old man was faulty, since the old man also was not a native speaker of English. In contrast, he can be sure Larry's American English is authentic, because he can take it from the two hundred pages of notes. But at another level, if the old man, Ramirez, represents Puig's father, then we remember that his father is one of those first generation Argentinians, an exile in that sense, who had to leave his spontaneous native Catalan behind and speak faultily in the language of his newly adopted country. Larry, who I am suggesting in some ways in the novel replaces the son who was killed, represents the children of those immigrant parents who speak the new language fluently, having learned it directly from the culture—but it is a language of popular jargon. Ramirez irritates Larry by constantly asking him the meaning of words, and he does not mean the denotative meanings, which he can find for himself in a dictionary. He means, what do they *really* mean, what do you feel when you are using those words? At the same time, he criticizes Larry for speaking in the glib jargon of Freudian psychoanalysis.

Though Puig denies that he is himself present in the novel, it is not difficult to see parts of him in both characters. Like Ramirez, he is an exile who must leave behind his own language and try to learn the real meaning of words in his new language: "Before, language was a vehicle for psychology and manners, a language of which I had all the keys; now I had all the facts of a language [English] of which I did not have the keys" (Corbatta, 620). It is Puig, not his father, who actually came to New York an exile from the repressive Argentine government. It is Puig who, ten years older than this young man, may well have had something like a father/son relationship with him, and it is Puig as author who, like Ramirez in the novel, voraciously seeks to learn everything about the young man, about his past life, about how he feels, about what words mean to him. "It is a case that I couldn't let escape: he is a very emblematic person, very interesting" (Corbatta, 620). In taking the two hundred pages of notes, Puig was taking the life and the language for the purposes of his novel. It is interesting to note that Larry at one point in the book says to Ramirez, "You parasite."[11]

The old man is indeed like Puig's father temperamentally. As we saw with Berto, who represented Puig's father in *Betrayed by Rita Hayworth*, Ramirez spent so much time with his work that he had almost no time for his wife and his son. Because of the pressure on him, he was extremely irritable, and if he was disturbed, particularly if he was awakened from his nap, he flew into a violent rage that frightened others in his family. Like Berto/Puig's father, Ramirez was puzzled by his son, who was bright but not quite satisfactory, not manly enough. As Larry comes more and more to stand in for his real son (whose existence and destruction he has repressed), Ramirez fantasizes for Larry heroic adventures and a successful marriage, and then is bitterly disappointed when the real Larry does not live up to his fantasies. Under stress he flies into unreasoning rages against Larry.

At this point, Larry begins in certain ways to represent Puig—the son of this father. The old man, while imprisoned, had kept a clandestine notebook in this fashion: he had with him some books of French literature. He put numbers above certain words, and if you took those words out and arranged them in numerical order, they made sentences that revealed his thoughts and told of the events of his life. Sometimes he did not keep his journal word by word, but when he found a whole passage in the French that approximated what he wanted to say, he would mark that entire passage. Larry thought that if these words were transcribed, the resulting volume would be significant, and he got publishers interested in the venture.

The French in the novels says only approximately what Ramirez needs to say. Similarly, the immigrant Argentinians, deracinated, imprisoned in their alien culture, must shape their lives in an approximate fashion out of the words of the borrowed culture, out of a language of which they do not have all the "keys," out of words whose dictionary meanings they know, but without the knowledge about how to feel while uttering them. Puig, writing his novels, uses the words of that borrowed culture—the songs, the movies, the romances—transcribing them in such a way as to draw out their significance.

In taking these materials Puig himself in a sense is stealing, he too is a parasite. Ramirez draws back from Larry in fury, refuses him permission to use the notebooks, and accuses Larry of stealing his life for his own profit and gain and of not sharing any of it with Ramirez. At the base of his attack is his concern that Larry, with his transcribing, is digging up a part of the past that Ramirez has blotted out, a part of his life that he doesn't want to think about—his failures and the destruction of his family.[12]

Larry is hiding from his own failures. He has not been a "success" in life, has not advanced in his career and made lots of money as his culture has told him he should (here paralleling Puig at this age). More painfully, his marriage with his childhood sweetheart has collapsed, she has become an alcoholic, and they are divorced. He has fallen into solipsistic despair. He explains his failures in terms of popular Freudian psychology, through Oedipus complexes, incest fears, and so on, though Ramirez constantly reminds him that this explains nothing, that it is just a vocabulary to hide behind (as was, of course, the French in his code). He is partially right, and yet the popular psychology explanation is also partially right. Even as they are debating it, they are acting out—even if only in fantasy—an oedipal conflict for the attention of one of the nurses to whom they are both attracted. In the end Ramirez gets the nurse to take his part and to prevent Larry from getting possession of the notebooks after he dies.

The novel ends hopefully. Larry has already profited by transcribing the notebooks, in the sense that he has unblocked himself and is able to function in the real world. The father figure, too damaged by his culture to be able to act consciously, has nonetheless given his son an inheritance. Larry, with his shrewd mind and good education, will become a labor organizer. Before, he had loved in an aesthetic way the writings of Marx and Engels, but now he wants the practice as well. The parallels abound between Larry and Puig, who, transcribing the lives of the preceding generation in their own borrowed words and borrowed culture, saw his way through his own personal problems, adumbrated in the first novel, and worked toward a position of looking outside himself to the problems of his people, of all people.[13]

Larry's language (reminiscent of Valentin's in *Kiss of the Spider Woman*) is often couched in commonly used Freudian and Marxian terms, revealing two levels of popular culture. There is a third level of popular culture in the novel. Larry and Ramirez share a Catholic upbringing, and though they both seem to have repudiated it, their religious base constitutes another system of myths and vocabulary affecting their way of perceiving the world. Larry and Ramirez are constantly acting out scenes together in which they take the parts of father and son. In one scene, Ramirez is God, old, dying, impotent, and Larry is Christ, who, much against his will, will be forced by his father to go down to the "sewer" of earth to set things right, now that God no longer has the power. Throughout the novel they have been competing, oedipally, for the attention of a nurse who, because of her astrological sign, they have nicknamed Virgo. The three levels of popular culture neatly dovetail at the end. While undergoing psychoanalysis, Larry had learned that he must stop lusting for his mother and transfer his libido to an individual outside his family, perhaps sublimating it to a love of society. As combination oedipal and Holy family, it is appropriate that God the Father wins out in the competition for "the Virgin"—that is, Christ's mother—and that Christ the Son is cast into the world to set things right—in this case as a Marxist union organizer.

IV. THE BRICOLEUR

*Al principio, más que nada, me interesaba el lenguaje de él . . .
pero traído de la mano apareció todo un historial.*

In the beginning, more than anything else, I was interested in
his language . . . but along with it came a whole history.

Manuel Puig, interviewed by Reina Roffé

In 1980 Puig moved his home-in-exile to Rio de Ja-
neiro. Just as when he had lived in New York he had met a
young man whose English and whose personality had
made so strong an impression on him that he had taken
pages of notes, and in the end written a novel about him,
so when he arrived in Brazil he met a young man whose
character and whose Portuguese struck him so powerfully that he began recording it.

On taking an apartment and making some improvements, I
had a mason come to work on my house. I opened the door
and a moment later realized I had a character on my hands,
because really the case was remarkable. It was a question of
someone of another age, another language, another social
condition, a young man who was, when I met him, in his thirties, very strong, with health to give away, and at the same
time there was something strange. He didn't name things by
their true name, everything was a baroqueism (todo era ba-
rroquismo), he had to modify or at least adorn the actual reality. Evidently it was a question of someone who wasn't com-
fortable with reality, otherwise he wouldn't have taken all this
trouble. He instantly produced an identification, and I
wanted to know the reason. I asked him if after work he would
put in an extra hour seated beside my tape recorder; and we
talked. In the beginning, more than anything else, I was interested in his language, I have already told you it was meta-
phorical and at the same time charming; it was a poetic country language of great quality, and I wanted to record it because
some time it could be that I had to work with this level of language and I wanted to see where its perfume came from. I

began my investigation for the language but along with it
came a whole history. (Roffé, 144)

The novel that grew out of this encounter is, in my
estimation, as perfect an embodiment of Puig's social and
aesthetic preoccupations as *Kiss of the Spider Woman*. I happened to be living in Spain in 1982 when *Sangre de Amor
Correspondido* appeared in the bookstores. I believed at the
time it was one of his best novels, a sort of culmination of
things he had been working toward. The amazing language was so much at the center of the book that I thought
it would be the supreme challenge to translate the work.
Now that I have seen *Blood of Requited Love* (1984) I think
the translator has been only partially successful. I will
return to this point.

Since this is to be the last novel by Puig discussed
here,[1] it is probably a good moment to begin with some
summary statements about all of Puig's novels. As a kind
of simplification, one could say that Western fiction has
undergone a shift from the chatty authorial voice of the
nineteenth century to an increasingly objective presenta-
tion in the twentieth century, with the author moving further and further away from the center of the work. But few
have carried this tendency to such programmatic lengths
as Puig. From the beginning (*Betrayed by Rita Hayworth,
Heartbreak Tango*) his effort has been to eliminate as radi-
cally as possible any sign of the presence of the author.
This has meant a scientific detachment in the photograph-
ically detailed description of scene, almost au nouveau
roman, with character revealed entirely through dialogue
or through interior monologue. The result is a sort of "su-
perrealism," a documentary objectivity so pronounced
that in the end it calls attention to itself and in a round-
about and ironic way becomes poetic (just as superreal-
ism in painting calls attention to itself through its very
flawlessness, calls attention to its surface at the very moment it pretends to eliminate the surface). Further supporting the scientific detachment of the narrative style,
the actions of Puig's characters often seem to fit into the

pattern of sociological or psychoanalytical case studies. Puig's initial style is carried even further in *Kiss of the Spider Woman* and *Eternal Curse on the Reader of These Pages*, where the characters are presented to us entirely through unmediated dialogue and with only such description as they themselves provide in their conversation. Towards the end these novels are supplemented by various documents: letters, police reports, a carefully researched essay on various theories of the origin of homosexuality. One motive may be to eliminate as much as possible the subjectivity of the author, which, overlaying the subjectivity of the protagonists, is just one more filter separating us from their reality. The characters must already experience their own reality filtered through the distortions of their culture and language. In this regard they are akin to characters in Peter Handke's novels.

Puig and the Austrian writer Peter Handke, two of the great innovators of contemporary fiction, are surprisingly alike in their fictional and social concerns. Both are linguists and citizens of the world. Both have a fascination with film, especially with the Hollywood film, and the romanticized American culture it reflects. Both deal in their fictions with middle-class characters who inhabit a semiotic maze of distorted and distorting language that traps them in the confines of a rigid society. The philosophy of both writers would run something like this: We perceive the world through the language we speak. The society, as an organism, creates a language not for the purpose of freeing people to pursue their maximum development but rather to subjugate people to its own needs. The language that best preserves the status quo of the society is the language that most frustrates the free-ranging development of the individual. The individual who can somehow elude the net of language is dangerous to the society—at least the society believes so—and so it uses methods, ostracism for example, to deal with offenders. In Handke's novels, his most sensitive characters can be destroyed by language, but sometimes, if they have superior linguistic abilities themselves, they can eventually rise above it and save themselves.[2] The more sensitive of Puig's characters are destroyed in the same way, but when his characters triumph (however briefly or ambiguously), it is, by some miracle, from within the corrupt language, by an act of personal creation revitalizing and somehow overcoming the falsehood in the language to construct something genuine.

In a wonderful way, the activity of triumphing over language either by rising above it (Handke's characters) or by staying within it but transforming it (Puig's characters) is paralleled in the language and the techniques of the novels themselves. In common with many recent writers, Handke and Puig make heavy use of pastiche. With Handke there are frequent parallels with, or allusions to, past literature and, as mentioned, Hollywood films. Also with Puig the Hollywood film is never distant, but his other allusions and parallels are to schlock and schmalz culture—soap operas, the tango and bolero, women's magazine romances, detective novels. Here is an important difference between Handke and Puig: where Handke quotes in order to deny, Puig quotes in order to revivify, to transform, and to make legitimate these banal forms. In keeping with this, in Handke's novels the language comes from without and bombards and buries the characters under its confusing welter. In Puig's novels the language is completely internalized by the characters and is not only the language of their environment but also the language with which they experience the environment, with which they feel and express their own thoughts.

In Puig's novels, the particular way the culture distorts his protagonists' sense of reality is by keeping them as children. The culture insists that pain and death do not exist, or at least not for them, and that what they want to strive for in life is the sort of sentimental romance embodied in Hollywood films. If the people, Puig suggests, are kept in a childlike state, then the power structure based on *verticalidad* can be kept intact and unquestioned; the paternalistic dictatorship at the top of the state and a tyrannic male at the head of each household keep females in subjection and force young males either into the mold of prototyrants themselves, selfish and spoiled deflowerers of the neighborhood's young girls, or, if the boys have some sensitivity, into effete homosexuality. All are compelled into the role of victim or victimizer. The cost is the inability, or the near inability, for individuals to love one another, because society has not provided the tools with which to express love. Rarely, and against all odds, love wins out briefly, as in the fully expressed love between Molina and Valentin in *Kiss of the Spider Woman*. Even in this example, the individuals can perceive each other only in terms of third-rate movies or of a cliché-ridden Marxism. Their love constitutes such a threat to the reigning hierarchy that the society must destroy them physically.

The young lovers, Josemar and María, in *Blood of Requited Love*, are nearly successful in their love, and that is why we feel pain in their eventual failure. The story—once it can be disentangled from the narrative—is quite simple: Josemar, in his late teens, starts dating María, a girl of thirteen. The setting is a small town in rural Brazil. María's father, a traveling salesman with a house in town, passes for rich in this area. Josemar's family and relatives are poor sharecroppers in the country, only a few generations removed from their wild Indian past. After three years Josemar and María separate and never really see each other again. For ten years after Josemar leaves, María has a nervous complaint and scarcely leaves the house. Finally she seems better, goes back to school to get a teaching degree, and is about to marry a wimp the parents have picked out for her. Josemar is working as a builder in the big city, has evidently been married briefly and unsuccessfully, and now pays a large part of his small income for child support. He seems on the point of falling into the despair and drunkenness that overtook his father. It is at this point, ten or so years after their separation, that each tries to work out what happened.

It is the oblique way the novel is told to us that marks it as Puig's, though on the surface it is anomalous because, for almost the first time in Puig, there is a narrator (not counting the pastiche narrations of *The Buenos Aires Affair* and *Pubis Angelical*). The narrator resembles that chatty nineteenth-century omniscient author, except that he is so unreliable—perhaps exaggerating the subjectivity of the standard authorial voice—that only the most careful reading can ferret out when he is telling the truth. The narrator turns out to be Josemar himself, telling his own story in the third person. And, quite impossible to explain in any naturalistic way, the voice or consciousness of María is also present—though the two people are physically separated by miles. Because of her mental and emotional trauma, she cannot remember with any certainty what happened, and she asks him to tell her, but he gives the version of the story his society has programmed him to give, distorted by the clichés and vulgar values of that society. The real story is hidden somewhere behind the words. In his narration of the story, he casts himself in the role of one of Puig's macho characters. He had blown into town in his Maverick, wearing the latest style duds, had become the incredible star of the town soccer team, and of course has all the women he wants. On the night before he is going to the big city to escape domestic entrapment and to meet his high destiny, he takes María to a hotel and deflowers her brutally, and in the scene there is blood all over and she is screaming with pain but also is delirious with pleasure. No, in a different version he takes her out to the woods and bangs her repeatedly, or no, it's in a shed behind his house where it happens, or standing up against a tree in her garden. María tries desperately to remember that feeling of pain, but she cannot.

The truth begins to come out. Despite his tough and banal talk, Josemar (who never had a car, who, being from the country, was not allowed to play on the town soccer team) is virginal and innocent, and his decency makes him the patsy of every victimizer. In fact he had never had sex with María or with the young girl across the street who threw herself at him. He had left town actually in order to prove himself. María's parents had broken them up because he was not rich or educated enough for their daughter. And more than anything, though it takes him a long time to realize it, his own mother had broken them up, a mother who cared so little about him that when she sees him for the first time after an absence of a few years she doesn't even recognize him. At critical moments she had kept the young couple apart and had taken for her own use all the money he had tried to save so he would be rich enough to win María.

The telling is the pleasure of the novel, as it winds round and round the day Josemar left María, and the readers and the characters try to learn what actually happened. Here is the challenge for the translator, to get the voice right. The translator is good at catching the banality of the words, the clichés, but less successful at catching the poetry of the *palabrotas*, the swearing, that can go on endlessly and fluently in Spanish but seems only awkward or impoverished in English. The translation is least successful at capturing a (probably fantasized) scene in which Josemar has a long conversation with his black brother-by-adoption, Zilmar, about whether you can make love when you are starving. The language, the chaffing back and forth between the two young men, is brilliant in the original; it is wooden in the English. Perhaps in the original it is so close to a kind of poetry that it is inevitably that which is lost.

I have read Puig's novels in Spanish and in English (*Eternal Curse* was written originally in English). Many were translated by Suzanne Jill Levine, and those I have read in her translation seem to give me the same tone and feel I get from the original. I am far from a scholar in this matter, but that seems to me to be what is desired in a translation. But let me make this suggestion. Because Puig so often is writing in dialogue, and even descriptive passages are written in close imitations of popular speech, the vocabulary he uses is small and complex sentences are rare. He is comparatively easy to read in Spanish, and I recommend that anyone familiar with the language try him in Spanish. The rewards, especially with this last novel, are considerable.[3]

The villain of the novel seems to be the rigid social system that separates the lovers, causing María's parents to forbid Josemar in their house and finally to forbid her to see him, ostensibly because he is poor, uneducated, and an Indian (in fact he is the product of his mother's liaison with a rich and very handsome white landowner). He himself feels deeply inferior to María for these reasons and strives to educate himself and to make money. But along with the social stratification is the autocratic rule by the parents, for María's father absolutely determines her fate and, in the case of Josemar, his selfish mother exploits his love for her, breaking him up with María to keep his money to herself and in the end leaving him without a roof over his head. But as with *Eternal Curse*, though the society is implicated, finally the characters' struggles seem deeply personal. Josemar has become a builder and an electrician because María said that is what she wanted him to be, and she has become a teacher because of his worshipful attitude toward teachers (one of his greatest disillusionments is to meet, ten years later, his favorite grade-school teacher only to find her as easy to seduce as "a tame cow"[4]), but it is too late for them.

Here is Puig's, here is the novel's, final transformation, for as the end of the story rounds back to the beginning we realize we have not been reading social criticism or even quiet domestic tragedy so much as a sort of lyric poem riding on a wave of popular language—*palabrotas*, clichés, and banality—raised to the pitch of art. As a mason, a builder, Josemar is literally that *bricoleur*, that maker of myths out of the culture's shoddy ready-mades and out of his own disappointments and failures. It is the story of Puig's career as a novelist.[5]

V. EPILOGUE

At the beginning of his career Puig had attempted to put his life into a screenplay. He quickly determined that his essentially realistic themes fit more appropriately into the form of the novel.

> The unreal cinema of the 1930s—*Casablanca*, for example—reflects the dreams of the people of that epoch. That brought me to think that realism doesn't find its major expression in the movies. Realism, that is to say, the quotidian, doesn't work in movies because the picture doesn't offer the possibility of the page. The reader has a patience the spectator does not. . . . What movies produce is magic. . . . My novels continue being realistic. There are certain themes that are better for literature. (Mujica, 6)

At the present moment (1988) Puig has gone six years without writing a new novel. He finds he is no longer interested in realistic themes. "Now I like to work in the theater. My work, *Bajo un Manto de Estrellas* [Under a Mantle of Stars, a play] combines the real with the imaginary." And when he is asked if that means he does not plan to write any more novels, he replies:

> I confess I am in a crisis. I have in mind an unrealistic novel, but I can't find the voice. I am on the fourth or fifth draft, but with no results. And I don't find a theme that stimulates me to return to realism. (Mujica, 6)

In my study I have stressed the continuity of his novels, how themes, characters, techniques evolve or are transformed from one book to the next. I have done this to thrust into relief certain aspects of his writing. But I hope I have not left the impression that he repeats the same book over and over. I can think of no other writer who is so averse to repeating himself. Once he has a "problem" worked out, he leaves it behind, just as he left the village of Coronel Vallejos behind when it had served his needs, though another writer might have continued squeezing bestsellers out of it. It is quite possible, having said what he has to say in the novel, that he will leave that form behind for good, for the greater glory of the theater.[1] Even if he does come back to the novel, it seems likely that it will be to a very different kind of novel. In either event, these seven novels discussed here will come to be seen as a unit, a chapter in Puig's creative development.

NOTES

Notes for Chapter I: Art Out of Scorned Objects

1. Saul Sosnowski, "Manuel Puig: Entrevista," *Hispamérica* 1 (May 1973): 69. Hereafter cited in the text.

2. Ronald Christ, "An Interview with Manuel Puig," *Partisan Review* 44 (1977): 56. Hereafter cited in the text.

3. See, for example, George Yudice, "*El Beso de la Mujer Araña y Pubis Angelical*: Entre el Placer y el Saber," in *Literature and Popular Culture in the Hispanic World: A Symposium,* edited by Rose S. Minc (Upper Mountclair, N.J.: Mountclair State College; Gaithersburg, Md.: *Hispamérica,* 1981), 44, and Alfred J. MacAdam, *Modern Latin American Narratives: The Dream of Reason* (Chicago: University of Chicago Press, 1977), 98. Lévi-Strauss discusses *bricolage* in *The Savage Mind* (Chicago: University of Chicago Press, 1966), 16–36.

4. *The Buenos Aires Affair: A Detective Novel* (New York: Vintage, 1980), 102–3. Hereafter abbreviated *BAA* and cited by page number in the text.

5. "Encuentros con Manuel Puig," *Revista Iberoamericana* 49 (April/September 1983): 598. Hereafter cited in the text.

6. "Between 1869 and 1929, immigration was responsible for 60 percent of the nation's population growth." Peter G. Snow, *Political Forces in Argentina,* rev. ed. (New York: Praeger, 1979), 9.

7. Manuel Puig and Suzanne Jill Levine, "Author and Translator: A Discussion of *Heartbreak Tango,*" *Translation* 2 (1974): 35. Hereafter cited in the text by the name Levine.

Notes for Chapter II: Betrayed by Rita Hayworth

1. Even here we must be cautious. "This tablecloth alone gave me more trouble than the whole set of doilies, a full eight pairs" ([New York: Avon, 1973], 5), among the first lines of the novel, is not just talk, according to Jorge Panesi, "Manuel Puig: Las Relaciones Peligrosas," *Revista Iberoamericana* 49 (October-December 1983): 904. He claims that these words refer to the novel itself, constructed in two parts (or "pairs") of eight sections each.

2. Marcelo Coddou, "Complejidad Estructural de *El Beso de la Mujer Araña,* de Manuel Puig," *Inti* 7 (Spring 1978): 16; and Pere Gimferrer, "Aproximaciones a Manuel Puig," *Plural* 57 (June 1976): 21, both give long lists of writers who conceal their narrators. Coddou also gives us a useful reminder of the distinction between narrator and author: "We should not forget, however, that he who makes himself invisible, reducing his role to a recorder of voices, in attitude of total neutrality towards

what occurs in the fictional reality, is the *narrator,* not the author. 'The narrator,' Vargas Llosa has said, 'is someone distinct from the author, one more of his creations, just like the characters, and doubtless more important, even in the cases of an invisible narrator, because all the rest depend on this secret character' " (p. 17).

3. Indeed, we learn that Mita married Berto in the first place because of his close resemblance to a popular leading man in Argentine movies.

4. Julio Rodriguez-Luis, "*Boquitas Pintadas:* Folletín Unamista?" *Sin Nombre* 5 (1974): 54, n. 2, points out that though *Betrayed* and *Heartbreak Tango* both take place in Coronel Vallejos during the same time period, there are no characters in common between the two novels, so Puig was clearly not interested in producing a *comédie humaine.*

5. See a discussion of this in Alfred J. MacAdam, *Modern Latin American Narratives: The Dream of Reason* (Chicago: University of Chicago Press, 1977), 99. In fact, in choosing his form he has gone back not to the nineteenth-century popular novel but to even more vulgarized modern descendents of it. In an interview with Emir Rodriguez Monegal, "El Folletín Rescatado," *La Revista de la Universidad de México* 27 (October 1972): 25, Puig admitted, "I never read a folletín in my life, but I have seen a lot of serial movies and have listened to lots of radio serials."

6. Puig actually made an attempt to have the novel published in serial installments, but he could not get any magazine interested in the venture. See Monegal, "El Folletín Rescatado," 25. Hereafter cited in the text.

7. Stated in an interview with Reina Roffé, "Manuel Puig: Del 'Kitsch' a Lacan," in *Espejo de Escritores,* ed. Reina Roffé (Hanover, N.H.: Ediciones del Norte, 1985), 135. Hereafter cited in the text.

8. It is noteworthy that the place taken by movies in *Betrayed* in the second novel is taken by tangos, boleros, and soap operas. Rodriguez-Luis, *Boquitas Pintadas,* 55, writes, "In place of . . . *Blood and Sand,* which inspired the title of *Betrayed* . . . we have as ensign in the second novel a tango of Gardel, each one of whose extremely vulgar verses heads the successive *entregas* of the *folletín.*" (He is speaking, of course, of the novel in Spanish. The epigraphs to the episodes in the English translation were altered to be more meaningful to English-speaking readers. See Levine, "Author and Translator," 33-34). Puig says that these characters, who accepted the system, were less in need of the movies as escape. Also he pointed out that the "women" movies could be subversive of the culture (see Chapter 1 above), and therefore perhaps these characters preferred the straightforward machismo of the tangos. In an interesting discussion, Angelo Morino, "Tanghi e Pellicole Hollywoodiane nei Romanzi di Manuel Puig," *Belfagor* 32 (1977): 396-400, points out not only that Puig's culturally insecure characters went outside Argentina to adopt the culture of Hollywood but also that the form of the tango they listened to was an import. Though the tango originated in the bordellos of Buenos Aires, it was not accepted by the middle class until it went abroad, during the First World War, and returned to Argentina contaminated with European ingredients. As a sign of Puig's control over his

materials, the characters, plots, and words of the tango as it was reintroduced into Argentina derive from the French serial novel, or the *feuilleton!*

9. "La Sexualidad Opresiva en las Obras de Manuel Puig," *Nueva Narrativa Hispanoamericana* 5 (January and September 1975): 155–56.

10. I owe these insights to Morello-Frosch, "La Sexualidad Opresiva," 156, and Monegal, "El Folletín Rescatado," 27.

11. "*The Buenos Aires Affair* y la Estructura de la Novela Policíaca," *La Palabra y el Hombre,* no. 18 (April-June 1976): 43–59.

12. Puig, asked to comment on the outrageous title of his fifth novel, *Eternal Curse on the Reader of These Pages,* said there is a "certain poetics of bad taste that interests me. Part of the Argentine thing . . . is to have a taste for earnestness [sobriedad] that I do not share" (Roffé, "Manuel Puig," 141). For the reader disinclined to believe Puig would stick such awful jokes into the foundations of his most serious fictions, let me give still another, and worse, example. Gladys affects the hair style of a Hollywood star of the 1940s, Veronica Lake. Veronica Lake always wore her hair falling across, and concealing one of her eyes. A sick joke of the time is that she was missing that eye. In Gladys's case—making the sick joke come true—she actually is missing that eye. These jokes, of course, are a part of the pop culture materials out of which Puig fashions his novels.

13. "Mimesis and the Motive for Fiction," *TriQuarterly* 42 (Spring 1978): 245.

Notes for Chapter III: Saved by Hedy Lamarr

1. Gimferrer, "Aproximaciones a Manuel Puig," 23, observes that this is also the first of Puig's novels to be told entirely chronologically, and Roberto Echavarren, "*El Beso de la Mujer Araña* y las Metáforas del Sujeto," *Revista Iberoamericana* 44 (January-June 1978): 65, points out that because of the limited locus and the short period of time covered the novel obeys closely the Aristotelian unities.

2. "El Mundo Imaginario de Manuel Puig," *Américas* (May/June 1986): 2.

3. For an example of life imitating art, while I was working on this chapter I happened to read in *Bloods: An Oral History of the Vietnam War by Black Veterans,* ed. Wallace Terry (New York: Random House, 1984), 294, an account by a Vietnam veteran of the time when he was held prisoner-of-war by the Vietnamese: "Man, did we miss the movies. . . . Bradley Smith, a Navy guy, could give you the best movie reviews you could ever hope for in your life. He would hardly miss a detail. Last almost as long as the movie. You could just close your eyes and see it."

4. *Kiss of the Spider Woman* (New York: Vintage, 1980), 41. Hereafter abbreviated *KSW* and cited by page number in text.

5. A number of commentators have discussed the footnotes in this novel. The best study is Yves Macchi, "Fonction Narrative des Notes Infrapaginales dans *El Beso de la Mujer Araña* de Manuel Puig," *Les Langes Neo-Latines* 76 (1982): 67–81. Macchi computes that the footnotes take up

approximately eleven percent of the novel and therefore need to have a significant narrative function to justify their inclusion. He points out the contrast between the ongoing narrative of Molina and Valentin (the supertext) and the scholarly footnotes (the infratext): in the supertext we must interpret all, and in the infratext, where all is dogmatically told to us, our interpretation is excluded. In the first place, Macchi suggests, the marked contrast enhances the mimesis of the supertext, makes it, by contrast, seem more real. A second function is that Puig's views on homosexuality, though implicit in the supertext, are so concealed that they might be missed by the reader, so in the infratext he is able to be explicit without disrupting the dramatic surface of the supertext. Since the supertext is connected to the infratext only by a randomly placed asterisk, there is no direct connection between the two texts. Once more, it is the reader who must make all the connections.

6. *Ver / Ser Visto (Notas para la Poética)* (Barcelona: Antoni Bosch, 1978), 35.

7. Gustavo Pellón, "Manuel Puig's Contradictory Strategy: Kitsch Paradigms versus Paradigmatic Structure, in *El Beso de la Mujer Araña* and *Pubis Angelical,*" *Symposium* 37 (Fall 1983): 194, suggests that Molina's "cooperating" with the warden in order to get food with which to feed Valentin parallels the actress prostituting herself to get food for the journalist. Hereafter cited in text.

8. I have taken this information from Ephraim Katz, *The Film Encyclopedia* (New York: Crowell, 1979), 679–80.

9. *Pubis Angelical* (New York: Vintage, 1986), 21. Hereafter abbreviated *PA* and cited in text by page number.

10. "Usos y Abusos de la Cultura Popular: *Pubis Angelical* de Manuel Puig," *Literature and Popular Culture in the Hispanic World: A Symposium,* ed. Rose S. Minc (Upper Montclair, N.J.: Montclair State College; Gaithersburg, Md.: *Hispamérica,* 1981), 33.

11. *Eternal Curse on the Reader of These Pages* (New York: Vintage, 1983), 105.

12. Jorge Panesi, "Manuel Puig: Las Relaciones Peligrosas," 914–15, suggests that what Ramirez has concealed in code is a rewriting of Berto's letter of reproach in *Betrayed by Rita Hayworth.* Berto's letter, Panesi points out, was a letter not *from* a father but *to* a father, as Berto's older brother stood in that position to him. It is significant, then, that the text Ramirez hides his letter in is *Les Liaisons Dangereuses,* and that the endangering relations are those between father and son.

13. Ibid., 904, n. 2, notes that Larry, having transcribed the diary and on the point of setting out on his career, is thirty-six years old, Puig's age on completing his first novel, *Betrayed by Rita Hayworth.*

Notes for Chapter IV: The Bricoleur

1. It is possibly his last novel. See below.

2. See my discussion of this in "With Peter Handke (In Spirit) in

Eastern Austria," *The American Poetry Review* (September/October 1984): 15–16.

3. Raquel Linenberg, "Léxico Argentino de *El Beso de la Mujer Araña,* y Algunas Apuntes Más," *Les Langues Neo-Latines* 76 (1982): 49–66, gives a useful glossary of Argentine slang expressions used in Puig's novels and describes the archaic use of *vos* for *tu* that is current in Argentina.

4. *Blood of Requited Love* (New York: Vintage, 1984), 141.

5. This chapter is a greatly expanded version of my article, "Children of the Power Structure," *American Book Review* (May/June 1985): 9.

Note for Chapter V: Epilogue

1. Puig's last two books have been collections of plays: *Bajo un Manto de Estrellas; El Beso de la Mujer Araña* [a play made from the novel] (Barcelona: Seix Barral, 1984) and *La Cara del Villano; Recuerdo de Tijuana* [screen plays] (Barcelona: Seix Barral, 1985).